Sports Titans of the 20th Century

There are and will be still more sports titans than are named in this book. With still a few decades remaining to the Twentieth Century and with the continuing improvement of athletic prowess, we will see even greater achievements in sports. Thus, the author offers just twelve sports titans now, with the promise of at least one more volume to come.

JIM BROWN

BOB COUSY

JIM THORPE

TY COBB

BABE RUTH

BILL TILDEN

JESSIE OWENS

JACK DEMPSEY

BABE DIDRIKSON ZAHARIAS

MAURICE RICHARD

WILLIE MAYS

RED GRANGE

SPORTS TITANS

TITANS

of the 20th CENTURY

by Al Silverman

G. P. Putnam's Sons   New York

FOUNDED 1838

GPPS

Jesse Owens

For My Mother and Father

Library of Congress Catalog Card Number: 68-15080
PRINTED IN THE UNITED STATES OF AMERICA
10 up

Contents

Introduction   7

Jim Thorpe   11

Babe Ruth   29

Jack Dempsey   51

Jim Brown   71

Ty Cobb   89

Bob Cousy   105

Jesse Owens   124

Bill Tilden   137

Maurice Richard   154

Babe Didrikson Zaharias   171

Willie Mays   184

Red Grange   203

Index   222

Babe Ruth

Introduction

In Greek mythology, Titan was the name of an ancient race of Gods, a very formidable race of Gods. They were the children of Uranus (Heaven) and Gaea (Earth) and they were blessed with incredible strength. One member of the Titan family was Atlas, who bore the world on his shoulders. Another was Prometheus, who gave fire to mankind. Thus it was perfectly logical for one of the United States Air Force's most trusted missiles to be named the *Titan*.

Thus, too, it is perfectly logical that the super sports heroes of the twentieth century should be known as titans.

It is an image we created for our sports stars. The first sports hero in America was John L. Sullivan. He was a titan who set the tone for all the others. It wasn't only that he could "beat any man alive," as he boasted. It wasn't just the thunder in his fists that made him the first great heavyweight champion. It was a combination of things—his murderous power, his awesome size, his swaggering, boastful personality. He looked and acted as though he could lift the world on his shoulders, and breathe fire. No wonder Teddy Roosevelt, when he went hunting in Africa, took along John L. Sullivan's gold-mounted rabbit's foot, for luck.

There were other titans in sports besides Sullivan before the twentieth century, but they never had a chance. There was a continent to tame and no time for sports. Our heroes then were soldiers like George Washington and Stonewall Jackson; explorers like Daniel Boone and Davy Crockett; outlaws like Jesse James and Billy the Kid.

It was the explosion of the industrial revolution that changed everything. Before 1840 we were largely a rural nation, a nation of farmers who had no time for sports. By 1880 we were first among the nations of the world industrially, and everything had changed.

For one, the population was shifting from the farm to the city, and city people were looking for the great spectator sports events. For another, waves on waves of European immigrants were flooding into America. These were people who, by and large, were used to sports; sports in the old country had been a part of their lives.

Then there was the thrust of the communications industry—the development of the telephone and wireless, of newspapers, magazines, radio, and motion pictures. These were the instruments used to burn into the sports spectator's mind the image of the sport titan.

But the biggest dividends of the industrial revolution were the money and leisure time it brought to Americans. Now people had the time, and the spending money, to go out and watch sporting events. The first professional baseball team, the Cincinnati Red Stockings, was organized in 1869. That was the beginning. By the turn of the century the enduring American spectator sports—baseball, football, basketball, tennis, golf, horse racing, track and field, etc.—had gained a firm foothold in the country. Sports was becoming an important part of our national consciousness.

It was natural then that, with the development of sports in our country, should come an adulation for the sports hero, the athlete who could run faster than anyone else, hit more home runs, shoot more baskets, score lower in golf, pass and punt and streak to daylight better than anyone ever dreamed. These sports heroes, these titans, became the real aristocrats of our democracy.

And the glory of our country is that there have been so many of them in this twentieth century. Just scan the sports titans of the last twenty years alone—Ted Williams, Joe DiMaggio, Stan Musial, Mickey Mantle, Bob Feller, Warren Spahn, Sandy Koufax in baseball; Otto Graham, Johnny Unitas, Jimmy Brown, Johnny Lujack, Gino Marchetti, Doak Walker in football; Wilt Chamberlain, Oscar Robertson, George Mikan, Jerry West, Bill Russell in basketball; Gordie Howe and Bobby Hull in hockey; Ben Hogan, Arnold Palmer, Jack Nicklaus in golf. We could go on and on, for the list is long and genuine and not just of the past twenty years. "Each generation of this land," Vice-President Hubert Humphrey once said, "has called its own cadence, written its own music."

And so it has: Joe Louis, the greatest boxer of his era; Walter Johnson, the greatest pitcher of his era; Paavo Nurmi, a superb runner in his era; Johnny Weissmuller, a magnificent swimmer in his era (and a magnificent movie Tarzan as well); Bobby Jones, an unbeatable golfer in his era.

But, wait. One other thing must be said for these gentlemen, and also for the twelve titans in this volume.

They were titans not because they stood out in their era alone, but because they transcended their era. They were men for *all* seasons.

Alas, we have room for only twelve titans here. The others must wait their turn. But we assure you that these twelve have the credentials. All of them made wondrous achievements to our folk culture. Some have died but their names live on. Their records, their achievements, speak to our age and will speak to our children's age. All are sports immortals. All are of the heritage of that ancient race of Gods who held up worlds and breathed fire.

And all were among the most potent entertainers of the century. They gave good and dramatic performances. They gave fun and relaxation and meaning to life in the twentieth century. Yes, they wrought miracles, but they did more. They made the good times a little better and the bad times not quite so bad. And what more can we ask of them.

AL SILVERMAN

Ardsley, New York

Jim Thorpe

IT WAS either my junior or senior year of high
school, I don't remember which, but I have never
forgotten that morning.

We were in a gym class, working the parallel bars,
climbing the ropes, doing all that gymnastic jazz, when
our teacher, Tom Whelan, suddenly appeared with a
stranger. The man was wearing a black, nondescript
overcoat and he held a brown felt hat in his hand.
Tom Whelan blew the whistle that dangled from his
neck.

"Come over here a minute, fellas. I want you to
meet someone."

We moved in and got a closer look at the stranger.
He didn't seem very tall and because of the coat we
couldn't tell about his build, but he looked heavy. He
also looked ill. His face had a pasty, yellow-brown pal-
lor. His hair was thick and flecked with gray. The
other features of his face gave a feeling of raw, cruel,
but used-up power—the close, slit eyes, the broad,
bashed-in nose, the thick, twisted lips, and protruding
jaw. But his face was softened by a sheepish smile, a
smile that seemed to say: Sorry to take up your time,
boys, but it's not my doing.

"Fellas," Tom Whelan was saying, "I want you to

11

meet a good friend of mine. But more than that, I want you to meet the man I think is the greatest athlete this world has ever known. Jim Thorpe."

The stranger raised his hand in greeting and the smile broadened.

Jim Thorpe. The name was just faintly familiar. This was, after all, 1941 or 1942 in Lynn, Massachusetts, and our heroes were the local superstars—Ted Williams of our Boston Red Sox; Milt Schmidt of our Boston Bruins; Charlie O'Rourke, the All-America quarterback from Boston College.

Jim Thorpe? Tom Whelan went on to tell a little about his friend, about the Jim Thorpe who had won the decathlon and the pentathlon in the 1912 Olympics, about the Jim Thorpe who was a smashing fullback for the Carlisle Indians, then the professional Canton Bulldogs, about the Jim Thorpe who played seven years of major-league baseball. But all that had been twenty or more years back and Jim Thorpe had faded into a kind of limbo. How could we be expected to remember this man?

Tom Whelan finished talking and Jim Thorpe waved goodbye and moved out of the gym without saying a word. The whole thing could not have lasted longer than five minutes and then we went back to our chores—and Jim Thorpe went back into limbo.

But, somehow, the memory stuck, the memory of that brief encounter took hold and grew. And in 1950 the memory burst into our consciousness and we reminded ourselves, why, of course, we once met Jim Thorpe.

For 1950 was the year that Jim Thorpe came back to life. The Associated Press had conducted a poll and

Jim Thorpe had been named the greatest football player of the half-century; the second greatest track and field star of the half-century; finally, the greatest athlete of the half-century. So Tom Whelan had been right. He hadn't exaggerated when he told us that Jim Thorpe was truly the greatest athlete the world had ever known.

He was, indeed. It is simply not possible to exaggerate Jim Thorpe's exploits. They defy exaggeration. The Sac-Fox Indian (named *Bright Path* by his mother) performed more miracles in more different sports than any other person in history.

Football.

In 1911 the Carlisle Indians met Harvard University, the defending national collegiate champions. Carlisle's sixteen-man squad came to Cambridge, Mass., as laughable underdogs. Harvard was three-deep, every man handpicked from the elite of prep school, then the spawning ground for college stars. On top of that, Carlisle's big man, Jim Thorpe, had spent the week on crutches trying to rest a battered leg.

Over 25,000 came to Harvard Stadium to see how high Harvard would score. Harvard's coach, Percy Haughton, contemptuous of Carlisle, started his second-stringers. It seemed, at first, like a logical move.

Harvard scored and kicked the extra point and led 6-0 (touchdowns counted for five points in those days). But Carlisle fought back. Thorpe, his leg heavily bandaged, kicked a twenty-three yard field goal. He kicked a forty-three yard field goal. He kicked a thirty-seven yard field goal. And Carlisle led at halftime, 9-6.

Percy Haughton, stunned by the Carlisle showing,

started his first-stringers in the second half. Harvard scored a quick touchdown and a field goal and led 15-9. And the Indians, who had absorbed a terrific beating, seemed to be through. But they were not through.

When Carlisle finally got the ball, Thorpe spoke gruffly in the huddle. "I'm gonna carry the ball now," he said. "If you can't help me, just get out of my way."

Thorpe carried the ball nine times for seventy yards and a touchdown. He kicked the extra point. And now it was 15-15.

Seconds left and Carlisle had the ball on the Harvard forty-eight and there was only one thing to do. Big Jim Thorpe prepared to kick.

The crowd was completely silent as the ball was snapped. Harvard's charging linemen swept in on Thorpe as he stood back there grandly by himself, took a step forward, dropped the ball, and hit it at the moment the ball touched the ground. The crowd was completely silent, watching enraptured as the dropkick went spinning high and deep, end over end, spinning between the goalposts, coming down finally as the three points were being recorded on the scorecard. Jim Thorpe's Carlisle Indians were victorious, 18-15. It would be Harvard's only defeat until 1915.

Track.

He could run the 100-yard dash in 10 seconds flat, the 220 in 21.8s, the 440 in 50.8s, the 880 in 1m.57s, the mile in 4m.35s, the 120-yard hurdles in 15s, and 220-yard low hurdles in 24s. He could broad jump 23 feet 6 inches, high jump 6 feet 5 inches, throw the javelin 163 feet, the hammer 140 feet and the discus 136 feet.

And so there was a scheduled track meet between

Carlisle and Lafayette University of Easton, Pa. Lafayette sent a welcoming committee to the train station to greet the Carlisle team. The committee was shocked to see only two young men get off the train, one short, the other tall and burly.

"Where's the team?" a member of the welcoming committee asked the big Indian, who was Jim Thorpe.

"This is the team," Thorpe said.

"You mean just the two of you?"

"Nope, just me. The little guy is the manager."

The next day Thorpe won eight first places, and the meet, for Carlisle.

Baseball.

The exhibition game took place in Texarkana, a town in a corner of Texas, Oklahoma and Arkansas. Jim Thorpe hit a home run over the left-field fence into Arkansas, hit a home run over the right-field fence into Oklahoma, hit a home run over the center-field fence, into Texas.

He excelled at whatever he tried—wrestling, lacrosse, basketball—anything. When he took up golf, he golfed in the 80's. When he bowled, he bowled in the 200's. He was an expert marksman, swimmer and boxer. Leave it to a king to recognize a king. After the 1912 Olympics, King Gustav V of Sweden said to Jim Thorpe, "You, sir, are the greatest athlete in the world."

But this was one king whose beginnings were humble. Jim Thorpe was born on May 28, 1888, in a two-room farmhouse near the Oklahoma settlement of Prague. He was born a twin. The other boy, Charles, died when he was eight from pneumonia. James Francis Thorpe thrived.

His father, Hiram Thorpe, a big man of incredible strength, was half Sac-Fox and half Irish. His mother was three-fourth Sac-Fox and one fourth French. The Sac-Fox tribe had once been a power in the area of Green Bay, Wisconsin and they were once led by a great chief. His name was Black Hawk. When he was seventeen he led a war party against the Osage and lifted his first scalp. At nineteen he led two hundred of his tribesmen against an equal number of Cherokee and killed half the enemy. Jim Thorpe's mother, looking at the ten-pounder, had a vision—that her son was the reincarnation of Black Hawk. The boy was called "Chief Bright Path."

And in that fertile environment, he flourished. Jim's father raised hogs, cattle, and horses, and Jim did his share of work. But there was time for Jim and his brothers to escape to the woods, to track game, fish with spears, and to learn the crafts of their forefathers. When he was ten, Jim bagged his first deer. By the time he was fifteen he could rope and ride a wild pony, and he was a dead shot with a rifle.

In 1903 the assistant superintendent of the United States Indian Industrial School, known also as Carlisle Institute, came to the Oklahoma Indian territory looking for students. One of the candidates was fourteen-year-old Jim Thorpe. "I want to learn the electrical trade," he told the superintendent.

"We have no electrical department," the superintendent said, "but you can learn to be a painter, a carpenter, or a tailor."

It didn't matter to Jim Thorpe. Carlisle, Pennsylvania, was another world and he wanted to see other worlds. So he signed up.

Carlisle was really a prep school rather than a college. Its classes went only to the twelfth grade, but many of the students were in their twenties and of the thousand students a few of the Indians excelled in football. As a result, Carlisle had to play a major college schedule. The small schools simply wouldn't play them.

Jim went to work as an apprentice tailor. Half his time was spent in schoolwork, half in tailoring. When he had a few extra moments as he finally did in 1906, he began to play football. He made the tailor's football team in the shop league. In 1907, he made the varsity scrubs.

The coach of the Carlisle Indians was Glenn Scobie "Pop" Warner, one of the most important coaches of all time. It was Warner who invented the wingback system—the single and double wings. This system called for an exceptional man at left halfback, a man who could block, who could sweep around ends and smash through the middle, someone who could punt, and run, and hit. Soon enough, Pop Warner discovered that Jim Thorpe was his man.

Thorpe was a substitute his first year and he didn't like it very much. But when the regular left half, Albert Payne, was hurt in a game against Pennsylvania, Thorpe was sent in.

On one of his first plays, Jim took the ball and smashed sixty-five yards for a score, leaving seven Pennsylvanians bubbling on their stomachs. Later in the game he romped eighty-five yards for another touchdown. Pop Warner was impressed. "He had a natural change-of-pace even then," Warner later remembered. "He kinda floated by the defense. His reactions were so fast that sometimes you couldn't follow him with the eye. Punishment didn't mean a thing to him. He was fearless and he hit so hard that the other fellow got all the bruises."

By 1908, Jim Thorpe was a blocky young man with a broad face, a heavy jaw, and bushy black hair; clearly of Indian heritage. Clearly, too, he was an athlete of promise. He played first base for the Indians, he was a crack hurdler, jumper and sprinter, he played all the sports he could. He was a tremendous all-around athlete when he concluded his first five-year term in 1909 and quit school.

On his way back to his Oklahoma home he stopped off at Rocky Mount, North Carolina, with two friends and they all signed to play baseball; semi-pro baseball. In those days many college athletes played semi-pro ball—played for money—under assumed names. Thorpe played under his own name. He played third base and was paid $15 weekly. Then he became a pitcher. His first pitched game was a 4-0 shutout against Raleigh. That year he won twenty-three out of twenty-five games for Rocky Mount. The Boston Braves heard of him and sent scouts, but Jim had strained his arm. He returned home in 1910 with no idea of the consequences of his brief baseball whirl.

In the fall of 1911, Thorpe received a letter from Carlisle. It was from Pop Warner. In it, Warner told of the Olympic games coming up in 1912 in Sweden. "I think if you return to school," Warner wrote, "you have a very good chance of making the Olympic team."

So Jim returned to Carlisle, just in time for the

football season. In the school's opener against Dickinson College, Thorpe played just seventeen minutes. He scored seventeen points. In the next game against Mt. St. Mary's he scored three touchdowns. On October 15 against Georgetown, Thorpe scored on a forty-five yard run. Then Carlisle began the major portion of its schedule, first against the University of Pittsburgh.

Before that game, the big-city newspapers in the East had been reserved about Thorpe. They wrote that he was making a name for himself against minor-league competition. Wait till the big boys got hold of him.

Well, big boy Pittsburgh could do nothing with Thorpe, or Carlisle. The underdog Indians won 17-0. Jim Thorpe was the hero and one writer summed it up afterward, "The Red Man is all they said he was—and much more."

In the next game against Lafayette Jim averaged over seventy yards in his kicks. He scored two touchdowns and a field goal as Carlisle won, 19-0. Against Pennsylvania, he set up two touchdowns, scored another, intercepted passes, played a savage defensive game and spearheaded another Carlisle romp. Then came the Harvard game and the high point of the season for Jim when he kicked four field goals to hand Harvard the only defeat they would suffer in the next four years.

At the end of the season, Jim Thorpe was named to Walter Camp's All-America football team.

This was Jim Thorpe at his peak—6 feet 1 inches, 185 pounds, and built like a Greek God. He had only one flaw in his makeup. Jim Thorpe was lazy. If the weather was bad, he often let up. "What's the fun of playing in the rain?" he once said.

On the boat going to Sweden in the summer of 1912, Jim relaxed in a chair, watching out of the corner of his eye as his Olympic teammates sweated themselves into shape. Even when he got to Sweden, his practice sessions were vague. But he told everybody he would be ready when the time came.

In those days the big Olympic events were the pentathlon (five events) and the decathlon (ten events). They were Jim's meat, lots to do. He once complained to U.S. Olympic coach Mike Murphy that there wasn't enough action. "My God, Thorpe," Murphy said, "how many events do you want to enter?"

"All of 'em," said Jim. "What's the fun of watching someone else?"

And this is just about what he did in Stockholm. In the pentathlon no one was close to him. He placed first in four of the five events, losing only the javelin throw. In the broad jump he leaped 23 feet 2-7/10 inches; he tossed the discus 116 feet 8.4 inches; and he ran the 200 meters in 22.9s and the 1,500 meters in 4m.44.8s.

In the decathlon he was fantastic. He scored 8,412.96 points to 7,724 for the runnerup, Hugo Wieslander of Sweden. He won the shotput at 42 feet 5.3 inches; the high hurdles in 15.6s; the high jump at 6 feet 1.6 inches; the 1500 meters in 4m.40.1s. In the other events he was never worse than fourth—100 meters in 11.2s; 400 meters in 52.2s; broad jump, 22 feet 5.3 inches; javelin, 149 feet 11.2 inches; discus, 121 feet 3.9 inches; and pole vault, 10 feet 8 inches.

The high point of Jim Thorpe's life came when he

ascended the victory podium at the conclusion of the games. King Gustav was there. He presented Thorpe with a bronze bust in the king's likeness, and a huge, jewelled chalice, carved like a viking ship and encrusted with gold, silver and precious gems.

Jim was overwhelmed and all he could say to the reigning Swedish monarch was a gruff, "Thanks, King."

He returned to the United States a hero. There was a triumphal parade up Broadway in New York and Thorpe was met by President Taft who called Jim, "the highest type of citizen."

He went back to Carlisle for another season of football, the biggest football season of his life.

Al Stump wrote about the fabled season in *Sport* Magazine. "Jim Thorpe became the topic of the day. From the lounges of private clubs to crossroads cracker-barrels, fans marvelled at his ferocity. He played for fun, but he also made the game a battle without quarter. It was as if he was burning inside to prove something—perhaps that his people had been defeated only because they were outnumbered and out-equipped. In him, was combined an Indian's tenacity, cunning and reckless courage, and an Irishman's love of combat— the unbeatable parlay as he proved that season."

In an early-season game against Dickinson, the Indians had been unable to do anything against the strong defense. Repeatedly, Thorpe had to punt his club out of danger. Now he was back on his goal line to punt again. The Indian center passed the ball high over Jim's head. Jim raced back, retrieving the ball ten yards behind the goal. A wave of tacklers surged in on him. Thorpe just had time to put his head down and butt straight ahead. The maneuver proved effective. Bodies bounced off him. Jim quivered for a moment, then regained his balance. Two more tacklers came in on him. He sidestepped one, he stiff-armed another. Suddenly, he was free and running like a deer. Nobody could catch him and it was 110 yards and a Carlisle touchdown. That broke the game wide open and Carlisle won, 35-0.

He did almost the same thing the following week against Lehigh. This time he intercepted a pass on his own goal line, opened up his tremendous speed and simply outraced everyone to the goal line. Carlisle won that one, 34-14.

In Carlisle's 33-0 rout of Syracuse, Jim scored three touchdowns and set up two others. He then led the Indians to a 45-8 rout of Pittsburgh and so reached the big game of the year—Army.

The Cadets that year were rated second only to Harvard in the country. They had four genuine All-Americas on the team, plus a right halfback named Dwight Eisenhower.

It made no difference to Thorpe. West Point had never seen a football player to compare with the powerful Indian. In the first half Thorpe led the assault on Army in one burst carrying three Army men ten yards to the Army goal line. A few minutes later he threw six straight passes to his teammate Arcasa, the last one for a touchdown. (Yes, he could throw, too.) When Carlisle was on defense, Thorpe kept the team out of trouble with his booming punts and deadly tackles. Three times his tackles forced Army fumbles.

In the second half Jim executed what the New York *Times* called "one of the greatest runs ever seen on the

Plains." He fielded a punt near his forty-five yard line, veered towards the left sidelines, found himself hemmed in, reversed directions and broke for the right sidelines. Eleven Army players had a shot at Thorpe. "I give 'em the hip," Jim once said, "then I take it away." He did exactly that on that breakaway touchdown run. Unfortunately, a Carlisle penalty nullified the run. But it was remembered. Carlisle beat Army 27-6 and the New York *Times* was so aroused that its normally gray prose turned purple. "Thorpe," said the *Times,* "was resplendent in a galaxy of Indian stars."

Against Penn the following week, Carlisle was upset, 34-26, but through no fault of Thorpe's. Pop Warner remembered that "Thorpe gave one of his greatest exhibitions that afternoon. Once he raced eighty yards for a touchdown, as beautiful a piece of open field running as I ever expect to see."

Jim Thorpe's last college game was played on a field covered with ice and snow. But the weather could no more stop Thorpe than could his opponents. At the end of the first half, the Indians held a slim one-touchdown lead and Warner ranted at his players.

"This is Jim Thorpe's last game," Warner bristled. "You owe him a victory for all the games he has won for you."

The Indians went out fired up, Jim Thorpe just as fired as the others. He ripped off three touchdown runs, threw a twenty-five yard pass for another. Carlisle won, 32-0.

All in all that wondrous season of 1912, Thorpe scored twenty-five touchdowns for 198 points. And he was Walter Camp's super All-America for the second time.

Then the storm broke over Thorpe. A Connecticut newspaper printed a story about Thorpe's baseball activities with Rocky Mount. The Amateur Athletic Union investigated. Jim readily admitted to them that he had accepted the money. He told them he had had no idea that he had done wrong; the money, after all, had barely covered his expenses. It didn't matter. The AAU made its decision. Jim Thorpe was to be barred from amateur competition of every kind. The International Olympic Committee insisted that he return all his trophies and gifts. His 1912 Olympic records were wiped from the book.

It was a cruel blow for Jim but at the time it didn't mean that much to him. He was twenty-four years old, at the very peak of his athletic powers, and the world was at his feet. He would become a professional baseball player. It was as easy as that.

And so it was, except that Jim Thorpe's professional baseball career did not quite live up to the Thorpe image. Five major-league baseball clubs wanted him. John McGraw, manager of the New York Giants, wanted him the most. "The fans will pay just to see the Indian take batting practice," McGraw told a friend. He offered Thorpe $5,000 for signing with the Giants. Jim accepted.

Jim had many of the natural attributes necessary for a pro. He could hit the long ball and he had a strong throwing arm. He had confidence. But there were other things that worked against him in baseball. Maybe it was the fact that baseball was not a contact sport. Maybe it was the slower tempo of the game.

Whatever it was, Jim's easygoing soul chafed at the discipline required in baseball. He became bored. Fun-loving always, he tried to establish physical contact in the game by roughhousing with his teammates.

One day in the outfield Thorpe began a playful tus-sle with Giant pitcher Jeff Tesreau. Thorpe finally pinned him with an armlock. The next day Jeff was unable to pitch because of a sore arm.

"I know how you got that sore arm," McGraw raged. "I saw you wrestling with that big Indian yes-terday." McGraw warned Thorpe to stop the non-sense. Jim just grinned that childlike grin at McGraw.

Jim became a part-time outfielder with the Giants. In some stretches he hit over .300, but McGraw always benched him in favor of someone else. One day Thorpe broke up a game with a triple against Grover Cleveland Alexander. A few days later, he was benched. John McGraw always said, in his own de-fense, that Thorpe couldn't hit the curve ball. But it was more than that. There was always the clash of per-sonalities between the two. McGraw demanded disci-pline and obedience from his players. Thorpe could give neither.

And so he drifted from the Giants to Cincinnati to the Boston Braves and then into the minor leagues. But it was all right for Thorpe. There was still foot-ball.

In 1915 professional football was about to be re-vived in Canton, Ohio. Thorpe was signed at $500 a game as player-coach. And he drew the crowds. One day, Thorpe played against the Massillon (Ohio) Tigers. The Massillon star was the end, Knute Rockne. Thorpe decided to test Rockne right away.

The first two times he carried the ball, he carried right at Rockne. Both times, Rockne cracked him to the ground for a loss. "You shouldn't do that to Jim," said Thorpe. "Look at those people who paid to see old Jim run."

"Well, go ahead and run—if you can," said Rockne with a big grin.

On the next play the grin froze on Rockne's face. Thorpe swung wide, then collided with Rockne, collided with knee, elbow and stiff-arm. He left Rockne in the dust and went sixty yards for the touchdown. As he trotted back to his position, Jim noticed Rockne walking groggily off the field. Jim came over.

"Nice work, Rock," he said. "You sure let old Jim run."

Jim played professional football for fifteen years. He played for Canton, for the Portsmouth Spartans, for the Rock Island Independents, for the Chicago Cardinals, for the New York Giants (where he was mostly a punter). He played as long as he could because, as it became increasingly apparent to him, after sports there was nothing left.

When he was forty-one years old he came to Pittsburgh with a semi-pro team. He was puffed out and his legs were stiff and old from too many batterings, but he was still trying. He carried the ball on one play and was hit at the line of scrimmage and a fan hollered at him:

"Throw the bum out! Whoever said he was an All-American?"

Jim Thorpe heard the crack and his tired, seamed face split in a wry grin.

But he was finished. The last years of his life were

sad years. He married three times. He drifted all over the country in search of work. When he could trade in on his name—in carnival shows, in bit parts in Hollywood—he did. When he couldn't, he went to work as a house painter or a laborer on a rockpile. In the 1932 Olympics at Los Angeles, Jim didn't even have the price of admission.

After the Associated Press named him the greatest athlete of the half-century in 1950, there was a brief Jim Thorpe revival. He received speaking engagements from around the country, and a movie was made based on his life. But the glory was gone and though it touched him in those last years to be remembered once more, he was touched also with sadness because of the way his life had turned out.

He died of a heart attack in a trailer camp in 1953. He was sixty-four years old and old Pop Warner echoed the feelings of most people who remembered Jim Thorpe. Said Warner, saddened by the news of the Indian's death, "I've never had or seen an athlete to compare with Jim Thorpe."

That estimate holds up today.

Babe Ruth

My voice may be loud above the
crowd,
And my words just a bit uncouth,
But I'll stand and shout till the
last man's out:
There was never a guy like Babe Ruth!

JOHN KIERAN was America's most erudite sportswriter when he wrote those lines in 1927, and in
1927 Babe Ruth could only be described in poetry.

For 1927 was the year of the Ruth, the year of the
sixty home runs, the year of triumph after triumph,
from opening day to the last day of the World Series,
with the New York Yankees smashing the Pittsburgh
Pirates for the fourth straight time and the Babe leading the way with two hits, one a home run, and three
runs batted in.

He was thirty-two years old in 1927. He weighed
240 pounds and carried all that weight on pipestem
legs, but he could still catch fly balls in the outfield,
and throw with deadly accuracy, and run faster than
people gave him credit for. And he could still hit. Oh,
how he could hit!

Twenty years later it was so different. It was Yankee

Stadium, 1947, a crowd of 70,000 on hand and Babe Ruth, now fifty-two, and dying, standing in front of the microphone at home plate. Babe Ruth, white-haired, his huge frame shrunk to half its size, his camel's hair polo-coat hanging limply on the scarecrow body. Babe Ruth, still a national hero, at the microphone and the voice coming out of him in a shocking, hoarse whisper:

"Thank you very much, ladies and gentlemen. You know how bad my voice sounds. Well, it feels just as bad. You know, this baseball game of ours comes up from the youth, the only real game, I think, in the world, baseball. . . . There's been so many lovely things said about me and I'm glad that I've had the opportunity to thank everybody."

Recently, I played that speech back, played it back on a long-playing record, and my eight-year-old son hid his face behind the record album because he didn't want anyone to see the tears that had formed in his eyes.

Why should that little speech cause such a reaction? Babe Ruth is just a name to my sons. He is, really, just a name to me because I never saw him play baseball. But the name is enough. George Herman Babe Ruth. The name, and with it, the legend, has been handed down from father to son, from generation to generation. It means something special to my son, as it will probably mean something special to my son's son fifteen years from now.

The legend surely didn't come just from Babe Ruth's achievements—from the sixty-one baseball records he held or shared by the time he had finally retired in 1935. Nor from the 714 home runs he hit in his long career. The setting of records was only part of it. The legend of Babe Ruth came from something deep within the man and something deep within ourselves, the one nurturing the other. And this is what must be examined in order to make sense of the legend.

The legend began badly. It said that Ruth was not his real name. But it was. He was born in Baltimore on February 6, 1895, and on his birth certificate was the name—George Herman Ruth, Jr. Baseball historian Lee Allen, after much effort, uncovered the truth about Babe Ruth's beginnings. In his *The American League Story,* Allen writes, "Ruth's paternal grandfather was John A. Ruth, the first of three men by that name, and in 1873 he founded a lightning rod business. He had at least two sons, George Herman, who was Babe's father, and John A. Jr."

Babe's mother was Kate Schamberger and George Herman Ruth Jr. was born at the home of her father. There were seven other children in the family, but only two lived to become adults.

Babe's father was a saloonkeeper and neither his father nor mother had much concern for their children. Both parents mistreated the youngster and it was a miserable childhood for George Jr. One day when he was six years old, he stole a dollar from his father to buy ice cream for his friends. When he got home that night his father was furious.

"Where's the money?" he asked. "What did you do with it?"

"I spent it on ice cream," the boy said.

"That'll be the last dollar you ever steal from me." He grabbed the boy, dragged him down the cellar and beat him with a horsewhip. A few weeks later, Babe

Ruth stole another dollar. "I wanted him to know he couldn't break me," Ruth said many years later.

His mother died in 1912. His father was killed in a brawl outside a saloon. In the years that they lived they were of little use to the boy. George Ruth had no real boyhood. He hated the traffic-clogged streets of the Baltimore waterfront. He hated the truck drivers who cursed the kids and struck at their legs with whips. He hated the police. He grew to hate all authority. He roamed the streets with a gang, stealing and fighting and defying authority.

In 1902 when he was seven years old he was put in a school for orphans and delinquent boys—St. Mary's Industrial Home for Boys. The school was run by the Brothers of the Xaverian Order, and there George Ruth learned the tailoring business, learned to play baseball—and also that there were good people in the world.

The good people to young Ruth were the Brothers who ran the school, particularly the Brothers who were keenly interested in sports. Athletics appealed to Babe Ruth, especially baseball, and so he became a catcher on one of the many league teams at the school. This was the start of his famous career. In his last year at St. Mary's he was a pitcher.

One day in 1913 Brother Gilbert, who was coach of St. Joseph's College, came to St. Mary's. He watched one of the league games and his eye was caught by a big kid in a blue denim shirt and overalls who was catching, lefthanded. The boy had a mask, but no other equipment. He was wearing a glove made for a righthander, which he wore on his left hand. When he got the ball, he whipped off the glove, tucked it under his right arm and rifled the throw to second. "And how he could throw!" Brother Gilbert recalled. "The ball was three feet off the ground going through the box and three feet off the ground when it got to second base. I knew that with an arm like that, he could be made into a pitcher."

Then Brother Gilbert watched the youngster bat. "The pitcher for the other side was a tall lean boy by the name of Tom Padget. Padget pitched the ball and Ruth hit it aganst the right-field fence. The next time up, he hit it over the center-field fence. The third time, he hit it over the left-field fence. The fourth time, he struck out. And he looked better striking out than he did hitting home runs."

It was Brother Gilbert who recommended Ruth to Jack Dunn, manager of the Baltimore club in the International League. Dunn came to visit "Big George," as Babe was then called, in February of 1914, on Ruth's nineteenth birthday. He liked what he saw. The boy was big, over 6 feet tall, 170 pounds and still growing. He had a mop of black hair, he already had that big chest and wide shoulders. He had those small eyes and the beginning of a round face. He was a hard-looking boy, but he was not ugly. Dunn talked to the head of the school and then agreed to become Ruth's guardian until he reached twenty-one. And he signed the youngster to a contract for the season of 1914, for a salary of $600. Babe celebrated by buying a motorcycle and riding it through the streets of Baltimore, his fingers to his nose.

Baltimore was training at Fayetteville, North Carolina, that spring and young Ruth enjoyed his first train ride. He felt as he had never felt in his life—the joyous feeling of complete freedom. And when he walked out on the ball field for the first time, tagging at Jack Dunn's heels, one of the coaches grinned and said, "Here comes Jack with his newest Babe." The other players, mostly veterans, picked it up and they got to calling Ruth, "Dunn's Baby." But soon they were calling him "Babe" with respect, especially after they saw him pitch and bat.

In the first intrasquad game, Ruth played for the "Buzzards" against the "Sparrows." His first time up, he hit a ball deep to right field, a 350-foot home run. It was 350 feet because one of Ruth's teammates, Rodger Pippin, who later became a Baltimore sportswriter measured it. Today, there is a marker in Fayetteville at the exact spot where Babe Ruth hit his first home run.

He became a starting pitcher at once. A month after entering professional baseball, his salary for the season was raised to $900. By July the figure was increased to $1300. He and two other players were sold to the Boston Red Sox for a total of $8,500. On July 11, that year he pitched his first major-league game, beating Baltimore, 4-3. But he finished the season in Providence after compiling a 2-1 won-loss record in five games with the Red Sox.

He came on slowly that year. He hit no major-league home runs. But he did hit home runs for Providence, and he did pitch well, and in 1915, he came up with the Boston Red Sox and that was the real beginning of the most illustrious baseball career in history.

Bill Carrigan was the Red Sox manager and he welcomed Ruth. He put him in the Red Sox pitching rotation and he used him as a pinch-hitter. On May 6, 1915, playing at the Polo Grounds in New York, the Babe hit his first major-league home run—a modest smash into the right-field stands. On July 21 he hit the first of his many mammoth home runs. This one came at Sportsman's Park, St. Louis. It went over the right-field bleachers, across Grand Avenue and smashed a plateglass window in a Chevrolet agency.

But in those days it was Babe Ruth the pitcher, not Babe Ruth the slugger. He was green and crude. He telegraphed every curve he threw by sticking out his tongue. But it didn't help the opposition. He had the American League's best won-and-loss record, 18 and 6, with an earned run average of 2.44. He also hit .315 and helped pitch the Red Sox into the World Series. But he was a frustrated young man during that Series against the Philadelphia Phillies. Red Sox manager Bill Carrigan used Babe only once as a pinch-hitter, and the Babe grounded out.

In 1916 he was magnificent in every way. That year he kept a suite at the Willard Hotel in Washington, D.C., for Red Sox road games. Once a Senator pitcher asked Babe how much it cost.

"A hundred bucks a day," Babe said.

"A hundred bucks a day! How can you do it?"

Ruth grinned. "A fellow's got to entertain, don't he?"

Ruth entertained all right, but it didn't affect his pitching. He won 23 games against 12 losses in 1916 and his earned run average of 1.75 was better than anyone's in baseball. He also batted .325. Once again the Red Sox made the World Series, but this time Ruth saw action. In the second game against Brooklyn, he pitched fourteen innings and beat the Dodgers, 2-1. After a first-inning Brooklyn home run, Ruth was untouchable. He allowed only six hits in the longest World Series game by innings ever played. When Bill Carrigan went out to congratulate him, Babe snapped, "I told you a year ago I could take care of these National League bums, but you never gave me a chance."

Remember, this was 1916 and Babe Ruth had left St. Mary's school only two years previously. He was now twenty-one years old but still a child in many respects. He mistrusted people and hated to be needled. One day when the cruel humor of one of his teammates was too much for him, he raged, "If you don't let me alone, I'll kill you."

The teammate backed off. "I figured he might have a gun or knife," he explained.

Soon it spread through the league that Babe Ruth was a dangerous man. He did have a dangerous temper. During a game in 1917 when Babe walked the first batter, he didn't like the calls. He hollered at umpire Brick Owens.

"Shut up or I'll throw you out," Owens hollered back.

"If you do," growled Ruth, "I'll punch you in the nose."

Owens thumbed the Babe, and Ruth punched Owens.

He was set down for a few days but it didn't hurt his record. Babe had his second 23-win year in a row.

In 1918, the Babe Ruth legend began to take roots. It was the year that new Red Sox manager Ed Barrow decided to play Ruth in the outfield and at first base on days when he was not pitching. As a pitcher, Babe won 13 games, lost 7. In ninety-five games as a hitter, his eleven home runs tied for the American League lead, and he batted .300. The Red Sox got back in the World Series and it was Babe's finest World Series performance as a pitcher.

In the first game against the Chicago Cubs, Babe pitched a brilliant 1-0 shutout. At the end of the third game the Red Sox led in games 2-1 and the boisterous Ruth was so happy that he took a playful punch at relief pitcher Walt Kinney and smashed his left fist against the steel wall of a railroad car.

He went out and pitched the fourth game of the Series with the middle finger on his pitching hand swollen and painful. But Babe ignored the pain. He pitched and won his second Series game. He pitched seven and one-third scoreless innings before Chicago got two runs in the eighth. That made it a total of twenty-nine and two-thirds scoreless innings for Ruth, a record that was to stand until Whitey Ford topped it in 1961.

In 1919 the transition became almost complete. Now Babe Ruth was a part-time pitcher and a full-time hitter. As a pitcher that year his record was only 8-5, but as a hitter he batted .322 and hit twenty-nine home runs and that was more home runs than anyone had ever hit in one year. Now the Babe was the biggest drawing card in baseball. And that was when the Boston Red Sox decided to get rid of him.

It was a matter of money. Red Sox owner Harry Frazee was also a theatrical producer, and he was in a financial hole. So, in January of 1920, he sent Ruth to the New York Yankees for $100,000 plus a loan of $350,000.

It was like a marriage made in heaven—Babe Ruth and the New York Yankees. It was the beginning of the golden age in American sports which included Jack Dempsey in boxing, Bobby Jones in golf, Bill Tilden in tennis, Red Grange in football—and Babe Ruth and the Yankees in baseball. It was the beginning of the jazz age and in New York City in 1920 there was the jazziest combination of all—Babe Ruth and the New York Yankees.

In 1920 Babe enraptured baseball fans all over the country by hitting fifty-four home runs. Wherever he went he was the object of hysterical attention. And now, more mature, more in step with the ways of this world, more gargantuan in appetite, he lapped it up. On the road his Yankee roommate was Ping Bodie, but when Bodie was asked who he roomed with, he said:

"With Babe Ruth's suitcase."

The Yankees finished third in 1920 despite Babe's display but in 1921 they won their first pennant. Babe batted .378 and hit fifty-nine home runs but he was a mild disappointment in the World Series. The Giants won the Series. Babe hit a homer and batted .313, the best of all Yankee regulars, but he was lost to the team after the fifth game with a wrenched knee and an infected arm.

Those disabilities marked the start of the lowest period of the Babe's baseball career. Arrogant and as contemptuous of authority, as ever, Ruth and Yankee left fielder Bob Meusel formed a team to barnstorm the country. They did so against the wishes of Commissioner Kenesaw Mountain Landis and baseball law of that day.

The tour was a financial failure and then Ruth and Meusel were staggered even more. Judge Landis fined them their World Series shares—$3,362.26 each—plus their pay for the first month of the season, which they were ordered to sit out.

Babe Ruth was burning mad that entire year. Five days after getting back into action he tried to invade the grandstand at the Polo Grounds to get at a fan who had been abusing him. Cops, ushers and teammates had to hold him back and Babe was ejected from the game—the last time he was ever thrown out of a game.

Another day Ruth told teammate Wally Pipp that he wasn't putting out and they fought in the dugout until separated. On a road trip general manager Ed Barrow hired a private detective to keep his eye on the players. In Joliet, Illinois, Ruth and his teammates were photographed in a speakeasy, and Barrow fined every man in the photo.

Babe batted .315 that year, with thirty-five home runs. But in the World Series, taking a merciless tongue-lashing from the Giants, the Babe made only two hits in seven times up and the Yankees lost in four straight.

That winter at the New York baseball writers' annual dinner, a New York State senator delivered a speech begging Ruth to reform. "The dirty-faced kids in the streets of America look up to you as some kind of god," said the senator, Jimmy Walker, who was later to become the celebrated Mayor of New York. "Are you going to let those kids down again?" Ruth got up, tears streaming down his face, and swore he'd behave.

From then on, he at least tried. Whatever excesses he engaged in, he did mostly in private. After 1922 Ruth *was* more responsible.

On April 18, 1923, they opened "the House that Ruth built"—Yankee Stadium. It was a house that Ruth had literally built by the huge crowds he had attracted to Yankee home games at the Polo Grounds, and the huge crowds he had brought out on the road. And on opening day 1923, 75,000 New Yorkers jammed their way into the triple-deckered stadium built to hold 65,000. They had come out to see if the Babe could bounce back from that poor 1922 showing. They had come out to see if he had truly reformed.

Well, he *looked* reformed. He weighed 209 pounds, his lightest ever as a Yankee. His bulging chest and shoulders tapered down to a flat stomach. He was still the same old Babe in the face, with the pig eyes, the thick lips, the enormous head; that same old ugly face that represented beauty to so many people.

And the Babe showed them. In the third inning with Whitey Witt and Joe Dugan on base, Babe came up against Howard Ehmke. The count went to two balls and two strikes. Then Ehmke threw a slow ball aiming for the corner and knowing he didn't have to make the pitch too good.

For an instant the Babe's fifty-four-ounce bat froze, then moved in a blur and exploded against the baseball. The ball arched high over the Stadium and dropped like a howitzer shot into the right-field bleachers for a three-run, game-winning home run— Yankee Stadium's first home run.

Nobody could stop the Yankees that year, and nobody could stop Babe Ruth. They won the pennant by seventeen games and beat the Giants four out of five in the World Series. During the season, the Babe hit .393 and blasted forty-one home runs. In the World Series he bombed the Giant pitchers with three home runs—two of them in succession in the second game—a triple, a double and two singles, for an average of .368.

In 1924 it was almost as productive, except that the Yankees slipped to second place. Babe hit .378 to lead the league and hit forty-six home runs.

And then came the famous collapse of 1925.

It started early in spring training when Ruth pulled a groin muscle while sliding into base. He kept on playing because he was Babe Ruth, the greatest drawing card in the world, and his muscle kept tearing. And then in Asheville, North Carolina, on the way north, the Babe suffered his famous attack of indigestion.

They said it came from eating too many hot dogs and soda pop. Skeptics had other reasons for the collapse. Whatever the cause, it was real.

He was rushed to the hospital. He almost died. It took him eight weeks to get back into the starting lineup and by then it was too late for him and too late for the Yankees. He batted only .290 that year and he had a big fight with his manager, Miller Huggins.

Huggins felt that Ruth wasn't giving his best, that he was out of shape and dogging it. One day in St. Louis when Babe arrived late for batting practice, Huggins' patience snapped.

In the clubhouse he told Ruth, "Don't bother to uniform today."

"What did you say?" the Babe demanded.

"You heard me. And I'll tell you something else. You're fined $5,000 and suspended indefinitely."

"You'll never get away with this!" the Babe roared. "I'll never play another game for you. I'll go to New York and see Jake! You don't think he'll stand for this, do you?"

Jake Ruppert, the owner of the Yankees, did stand for it. Babe arrived in New York telling reporters that he would never play for the Yankees again as long as Huggins was the manager. But after an hour in Colonel Ruppert's office, he had changed his tune. Ruppert stood behind Huggins, the fine stood and Ruth rejoined the team and made his peace with manager Huggins.

In 1926 the Yankees were the Yankees of Murderer's Row. Lou Gehrig had moved into the lineup in mid-season of 1925. A rookie, Tony Lazzeri, had taken over at second, and the Yankees had the best outfield in baseball—Bob Meusel, Earle Combs and Babe Ruth. The Yankees surged to a pennant.

The Babe in '26 hit .372, led the league in homers, 47, and runs batted in, 155. And in the World Series against the St. Louis Cardinals (which the Cardinals won in seven games), the Babe hit three home runs in one game. The third was a majestic line shot that flew 450 feet over the bleachers in center field, and into the street—the longest drive in the history of Sportsman's Park.

And in 1927 everything came together. The Yankees won 110 games, lost only 44, won the pennant by 19 games. Then they killed the Pirates in four straight World Series games. As a team in 1927 the Yankees had a .302 batting average, one of the highest in major-league history. Listen to some of these averages: Ruth, .356; Combs, .356; Gehrig, .373; Meusel, .337; Lazzeri, .309. It was the year that Gehrig hit forty-seven home runs and drove in 175 runs.

It was also the year that Babe Ruth nailed down the legend.

It came on the next-to-the-last day of the season, September 30, 1927, at Yankee Stadium. Babe went into the game with fifty-nine home runs. He needed one more to break his own record. The Yankees were playing the Senators and the score was tied, 2-2, in the last of the eighth. Mark Koenig was on third base and Ruth was up.

Tom Zachery, the Washington pitcher, threw a one-and-one pitch. It came in waist-high and Ruth swung, and connected. The ball streaked high and deep and settled, finally, far back in the right-field bleachers. As Babe ran out his sixtieth home run, the happy crowd pitched paper and skimmed hats in the air. When Ruth took his position in right field. the fans stood up and pulled out handkerchiefs and waved them in tribute. Babe responded by turning to the crowd, making a series of smart military salutes, his face ablaze with happiness.

And now the Ruth was mighty and had prevailed. He was earning a mammoth $70,000 a year, and was drawing enormous crowds to the ballparks. People who had never seen a baseball game, came out to see Babe Ruth. The Yankees played exhibitions all over the country and they came out in droves to see the Babe. One day in Indianapolis an overflow crowd began to boo Babe after he had failed to hit the ball out of the infield in three times at bat. But on his fourth time, he hit one that cleared the right-field fence and the street beyond and, when last seen, was bouncing from boxcar to boxcar in the adjacent freight yards. Afterward Babe said, "I guess I showed them something. Make fun of me, will they?"

It was almost as much fun in 1928 as '27. The Yankees won another pennant. The Babe batted .323 and hit fifty-four home runs. He led the league in runs scored with 163. He tied Lou Gehrig in runs-batted-in with 142. And then he went on to his finest World Series performance.

He did it even though he was limping from a charley horse. His limp was so noticeable as he took the field in the first game against the Cardinals that a reporter wrote, "He looked slower than a decrepit turtle going uphill toward a soup cannery."

It wasn't quite that bad.

In the first game he hit two doubles and a single and the Yankees won, 4-1.

In the second game as the Yankees won 9-3, Babe hit a double and a single. But people were disappointed. Wrote Hype Igoe, "The Series won't really start until Baby Grand lengthens out those two-base hits of his."

In the third game which was played in St. Louis, Babe got two singles and scored two runs. But he also showed something else.

With the score tied 3-3 in the sixth, Babe on second base, Robertson singled. Ruth charged for home as the ball was retrieved in the outfield. The throw home looked as if it had Ruth. But Babe slid hard. The impact of Ruth against catcher Jimmy Wilson was too much for Wilson. The ball was knocked from his hand. The Yankees won it, 7-3.

In the fourth game, Babe unloaded. In the top of the fourth with the Cardinals ahead 1-0, Babe stepped in against Willie Sherdel. He whipped around and the ball soared over the right-field pavilion roof.

The Cards made it 2-1 in the bottom of the fourth and it stood that way until the top of the seventh. Then, with one out, Babe came to bat.

Sherdel slipped over two strikes on Ruth and the crowd roared. As Ruth stepped back in, Sherdel quickly shot another pitch through the middle of the strike zone. It was a "quick pitch," which was legal in the National League but not legal, so Judge Landis had ruled, in the World Series. The crowd, assuming that Babe had struck out, let out a mighty roar. But the umpire refused to call the third strike.

Sherdel and manager McKechnie raged at the umpire while Babe Ruth stood back and laughed. Finally, the argument ended and Sherdel went back to the mound. The crowd was now laying it on Ruth, but it didn't bother the Babe. Willie's next pitch was another strike, or would have been, but the Babe didn't watch it go by. He swung that mighty swing of his and drove it onto the right-field roof to tie the score.

In the top of the eighth he hit his third home run of the game, again on the right-field roof. But he was not finished.

With the Yankees ahead 7-2, the Cardinals scored a run in the last of the ninth and two men were on base with Frankie Frisch at bat. Frisch hit a high foul near the left-field boxes. Ruth, who had been switched from right to left during the game, limped madly for the ball. He had to run through a shower of papers and scorecards, which were tossed out at him from the stands. He had to run on his bad ankle. But he caught up with the ball, leaned over the side of the boxes and, with one hand, grabbed the ball out of a boxholder's lap.

In Ruthian fashion, Babe stepped back, bowed, doffed his cap, held the ball aloft, grinned and then ran to the exit gate leading to the clubhouse.

All in all Ruth had batted .625, still a World Series record. He had ten hits, including three home runs and three doubles in sixteen times at bat. He had scored nine runs and batted in four.

Where else could Babe Ruth go now, after two such seasons as 1927 and 1928? Where else could he go but down?

Mercifully, the descent was gradual. He hit forty-six home runs in 1929, forty-nine in 1930, forty-six in '31, forty-one in '32, all the way to 1935 when, forty years old, he finished his career in the National League with the Boston Braves, hitting his 714th home run.

And there were little peaks along the way. In 1929 he was married for the second time, to Mrs. Claire Hodgson, a widow. The marriage was a great success. In addition to being a devoted wife, she began to manage the Babe's finances, and to see to it that he would be solvent in his later years, which was something the Babe had never thought about.

Ruth had always felt, in fact, that when he was finished as a player, he could become a major-league manager. In 1930 when the Yankees finished third despite Babe's .359 average and forty-nine home runs, the Babe was upset that he was not named new manager of the Yankees. Instead, the job went to Joe McCarthy, whom Babe called "that Busher."

But he went on playing as best he could. In 1931 he raised his batting average to .373. And in 1932 the Yankees won another pennant and Babe hit .341. The most spectacular achievement of his twilight career in fact came in that World Series against the Chicago Cubs.

He was thirty-seven years old, he weighed over 250 pounds, his stomach hung like a balloon over those incredibly skinny legs. But he was still the Babe, still with the enormous power in his wrists and shoulders and back muscles. He also went into that Series with a grudge against the Cubs.

In mid-season that year the Yankees' veteran short-stop and Babe's buddy, Mark Koenig, had been sold to the Cubs. Koenig helped the Cubs clinch the pennant, but his new teammates awarded him only a half share of World Series money. Babe Ruth publicly called the Cubs "chiselers."

The Yankees won the first two games in New York to the joy of Yankee fans, but it was different in Chicago. Cub fans greeted the Yankees at the train station by throwing overripe vegetables at them. A crowd of Chicago fans later surrounded Ruth and his wife, spitting at the Babe and shouting profanely at him.

In the first inning of the third game, Babe smashed a three-run home run into the center field bleachers. As he rounded the bases the Cub players hollered at him, "Pot belly . . . if I had you, Ruth, I'd hitch you to a wagon."

The Cubs came back and tied the score. The fourth run came in when the Babe was unable to come up with a line drive. The crowd hooted; Babe tipped his cap and took a deep bow. When he came to bat a few minutes later in the top of the fifth, the crowd booed louder than ever.

But the old man was unafraid. Charlie Root's first pitch was a fastball across the plate. As the strike was called, Babe raised one finger. Root's second pitch was another strike, and this time Babe raised two fingers. Someone in the Cubs' dugout rolled a lemon toward home plate.

The Babe smiled, stepped out of the batter's box and pointed majestically to center field. The message was clear—he would now hit one into the center field bleachers.

Charlie Root was incensed and he put everything he could on the ball, hoping to blaze it past the Babe. But he didn't. The Babe swung from the heels, swung that mighty swing of his, and connected. The ball flashed out to center field, landing, finally, in the exact spot where Ruth had gestured, under the scoreboard more than 400 feet away.

There were no real peaks after that. His salary was now down to $52,000 and in 1933 Babe hit .301 with only thirty-four home runs. The next year he played only occasionally. He hit twenty-two home runs.

Late that summer Babe had one more conversation with Yankee owner Jake Ruppert. It was an embarrassing conversation.

Ruth got right to the point. "I want to manage the Yankees," he said.

Colonel Ruppert said slowly, "I know how much you want to manage this club, Babe. But this is a big job. You have trouble managing yourself. Would you go to Newark, manage our club there?"

"To Newark?" the Babe said. "I'm a big leaguer. I've always been a big leaguer."

"Then," Colonel Ruppert said, "I can't do anything for you."

That winter the Yankees gave Ruth his release so that he might sign on with the Boston Braves. The Braves, owner, Judge Emil Fuchs, wanted Babe as a drawing card and he made vague promises about a future job as a manager. Ruth was named assistant manager, vice-president, and player. But as a player, he wasn't doing much.

In mid-May he was batting only .170 and he wanted to quit. Judge Fuchs wouldn't let him. "Stick it out awhile longer, Babe. We need the extra revenue."

On May 25, Babe was in the lineup as the Braves played the Pittsburgh Pirates at Pittsburgh. In his first time at bat, Babe pulled one into the right-field stands for a home run. The next time he hit the ball into the upper right-field tier. In his third appearance Pirate manager Pie Traynor ordered his infield to shift drastically to the right, leaving only his third-baseman on the left side. Babe hit a single through the hole at shortstop for a third hit.

In his last time up, the forty-one-year-old Ruth renewed his youth. He hit a home run high over the center-field fence, the longest ball ever hit in Pittsburgh, his fourth hit of the day, his third home run. The crowd gasped and then stood—to cheer every step as Babe Ruth jogged around the bases for his 714th home run.

Five days later he held a news conference and in his deep, hoarse voice he said, "I have had three ambitions, to hit 700 home runs, to be in baseball twenty years, to play in ten World Series. I've done all three. As things go along in sports, you know, as days and years go by, us older fellows, we have to take a side seat to let the younger blood come in and take our places. You can't go on forever in sports."

You can't go on forever . . . Babe Ruth was through.

He still hoped that he might land a manager's job in the majors, but nobody came after him and he spent the years left to him waiting. He played golf, he made personal appearances, he was always in demand to appear at public functions. But no one wanted him as a manager.

In November 1946 he had begun to suffer terrible headaches. He went to the hospital. It was cancer, but they never told the Babe. He spent eighty-two days in a hospital. Then, in February of 1947, went home "to look at the river." That April he made his emotional public appearance at Yankee Stadium. It was Babe Ruth day all over the country and there was hardly a dry eye in the house after he had given his little talk, his voice now barely a whisper; his body, too, a whisper of what it once had been.

He came back to the Stadium once more, on June 13, 1948, the twenty-fifth anniversary of Yankee Stadium. He came back once more to hear the cheers of the crowd wash over him, as they had never washed over any other ballplayer in the history of the game.

Then he went back home and, eleven days later, he was back in the hospital. On the night of August 15 his wife Claire bent over to kiss him goodnight and Babe said, "Don't come back tomorrow. I won't be here."

The next day he was dead.

And he was mourned by the people.

Jack Dempsey

JACK DEMPSEY. The name explodes in instant recognition; it conjures up a vision: Raw, cruel power. Savagery. The killer instinct. The man in the ring with the simian arms, the hair thick and black, the nose recessed almost to the cheekbones, the hate in the flat black scowling eyes, and the two-fisted assault.

Jack Dempsey. The name must be defined as *fistfighter,* the fistfighter incarnate. There can be no other definition for the man who in 1950 was voted by the Associated Press as the greatest fighter who ever lived. He was. He did not have the grace of a Sugar Ray Robinson, he may not have had the left hand of a Joe Louis, or the technical perfection of a Gene Tunney. All he was, really, was a prizefighter, and it was enough. As a prizefighter, there was never any one like him.

In the whole history of the fight game, there have been but eight million-dollar gates. Jack Dempsey fought in five of them, within a seven-year span. He was, in the 1920's—the Golden Age of sports—the perfect man in his profession for his time.

But there was more to Jack Dempsey.

Here we are in the late 1960's and the name has not

been forgotten. The name still rings, still carries the meaning it carried when he was at the peak of his profession. How can this be? How is it that Jack Dempsey remains one of the few enduring sports heroes of American folk culture?

It all rests in the life of the man—in a life which is full of little twists and ironies. This was a man who was mostly despised when he was pursuing his profession. He had been accused of being a draft dodger in World War I. It was a false accusation but it stuck.

Further, in the ring he was the primeval fighter, not the gentleman. He was Jack Dempsey, a lean and hungry killer, the man who stalked Jess Willard, who split open Willard's face thirteen times while winning the heavyweight title. He was Jack Dempsey, who had punch, speed, stamina, a fighting heart and, above all, the necessary cruelty to excel. He was as lithe as a panther, and as savage, with one of the most awesome punching combinations the ring has ever known—a crippling right to the body (that sometimes flashed below the belt), a crashing left hook to the chin, and a finishing right to the jaw.

He was accused of being a dirty fighter, but he hadn't learned to fight in a YMCA gym. He had learned to fight in the lusty mining towns of the west. "He had," said one fight expert, "the most highly developed 'killer' instinct I have ever seen." He was Jack Dempsey, a killer with no heart, and many people despised him.

And then Gene Tunney beat him once, and once more, and suddenly the turning point occurred. It began after his retirement in 1927, continued through his comeback in 1931, through 1932, through eight

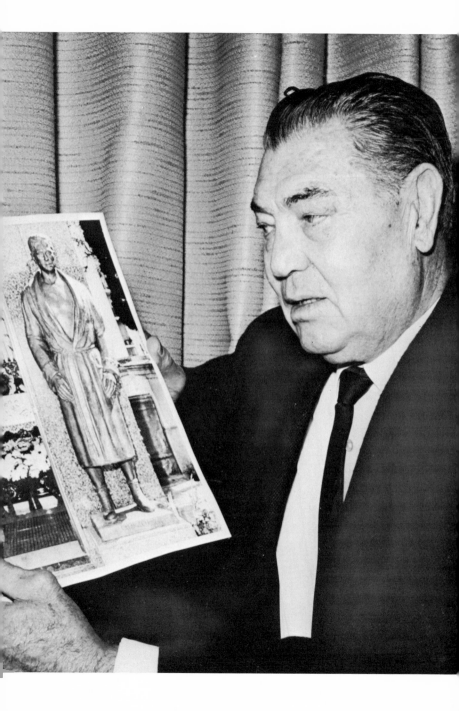

more years of retirement, until 1940 when, at age forty-five, he fought three more times. All through the war years, and then the postwar years, Jack Dempsey continued to grow in stature. Other boxers, other sports figures, lapsed into obscurity once their careers were over. Jack Dempsey was different. Jack Dempsey's name retained its potency. If anything, the name became bigger than ever. His image had turned around 360 degrees.

Time, of course, had something to do with the magic transformation. The cruelty had long gone out of Dempsey's eyes after his retirement. He was still remembered as the destroyer of Willard, Georges Carpentier, Luis Firpo—still remembered as the man who fought 148 times and knocked out 108 of his opponents—but the image had softened. A few years ago, Dempsey gave an interview and talked about becoming a medical doctor or a psychiatrist, about healing people, not maiming them.

"I think I could have done more for humanity as a doctor," he said. "Everybody in the world needs help and encouragement. If I do something to man, it comes back a hundredfold. You have to be a human being in the world. I'm no angel. Don't misunderstand me. But as I get older, I realize that it's only the good things you do for people that count."

This is the message that he has taken to the public in the years since his retirement. And he has always kept before the public. He has had a private life of course. He married four times. He raised a family. But he never strayed far from the public promenade. He has logged 100,000 air miles a year for many years. He has made personal appearances here, refereed boxing bouts there. He has promoted boxing shows. He has testified before congressional committees. He has lent the use of his name to various promotions. And when he is in New York City, his hometown now, he makes sure the public sees him by sitting at the table nearest the windows in the restaurant that bears his name on Broadway, so that people can go to the window and be rewarded by the sight of him.

On the streets even today, it is the same. People turn around to stare at the man now in his seventies, to nudge their companion and say, "Look, it's Jack Dempsey." When he moves out of New York into the country, he evokes similar reactions. He is still Jack Dempsey, the public figure, the hero.

It will be this way, if Jack Dempsey has his say, to the day he dies. It is the life he chooses, the life he loves, and no one appreciates it more than this man they still call the Manassa Mauler.

And this is why he loves it: as a boy, and later as a young man, his life was jagged and flawed.

William Harrison Dempsey was born in a two-room, one-story wooden cabin on the outskirts of Manassa, Colorado. The date was July 24, 1895, and he was the ninth child in a family of eleven children.

Celia and Hiram Dempsey, pioneer people, had moved their family from Logan, West Virginia, to Manassa on a $300 stake. Hiram Dempsey, who had originally come from County Kildare, Ireland, was a wanderer. Celia was Scotch-Irish, with a touch of Cherokee in her blood. She was ambitious for her children; not Hiram.

Those early years were struggling years for the Dempseys. Jack remembers driving to town as a boy with his father and buying five dollars' worth of staples to last them an entire month. He remembers hunting and fishing for food. "Harry" Dempsey as Jack was called then, and his sister Elsie, were the only Dempseys to have had as much as a grammar school education. Even at that it was an interrupted one, for Jack had to work as soon as he was old enough. He was a woodchopper in one village, a coal hauler in another, and a shoeshine boy in a third.

When he wasn't at work or school, there was time for play, and the play Jack liked best was fighting. All the boys in the Dempsey family liked to fight. The name, "Jack," became very popular in the Dempsey household.

Some fifteen years earlier a man named Jack Kelly, whose fighting name was Jack Dempsey, had become middleweight champion. He was a County Kildare man, too, so three of the Dempsey boys adopted the name Jack. They all wanted to be fighters. The oldest boy, Bernie, taught the younger boys, Harry and Jack. He taught them to punch, to dodge punches. He made their own punching bags out of sawdust and rags. They fought with bare fists or workmen's gloves stuffed with padding. They chewed gum all the time to make their jaws strong.

"We all wanted to be world's champion," Dempsey recalled. "I remember one day my brother opened a package of cigarettes and a little cardboard picture of Jack Johnson fell out. We all dived for it, fighting and clawing. I got it. I carried it around for years. He was the man I thought I'd have to beat."

There were other men—and other conditions— Jack would have to beat first. When he finished the eighth grade, he left home. He took to the freights with less than two dollars in his pocket. And he began years of wandering, years of working, and years of fighting. The work was hard work. He was a ditchdigger, he switched ties under steam shovels, he picked peaches for two dollars a day, worked as a bouncer in dancehalls, a loader in copper mines, a pick-and-shovel man in coal mines. And he did it all before he was twenty. His years as a desperate, hungry road kid were rougher than any heavyweight champion ever had to undergo.

Ned Brown, the boxing writer who knew Dempsey as well as any man alive, once told about some of Jack's early experiences.

"Like all hoboes," said Brown, "his cruelest and most relentless enemies were the railway dicks. He beat them up every chance he got. He had no choice. Some of them would let you ride in empty freight cars if you had a dollar to slip them—but most of them preferred to slug the hell out of you using the heavy clubs they carried. While you lay unconscious, they would take any spare change you happened to have on you."

Once, Jack and the other hoboes were riding in an empty freight car when they were caught by the railway dicks. All hoboes who had a dollar were allowed to stay on the train. Jack had no money so he was ordered out. He ran off into the woods but as soon as the freight train started, he ran after it and climbed to the top. But one of the detectives saw Jack, chased him, and finally cornered him in the last car. The detective clubbed Jack over the head and knocked the youngster off the moving freight.

That was the way it was for Dempsey as a young man, and after he became heavyweight champion he always had an answer for those who called him a tramp and a no-good bum. "Who would ride the rods when he could travel on cushions?" asked Jack. "Who would clean out spittoons to get the price of a meal if he could help it? Who would eat garbage if he could eat in the best restaurants? What man would be crazy enough to sleep in a hobo jungle, eaten up by bugs, worrying that it may rain in the night, surrounded by poor, broken-down old tramps who may go out of their heads any time at all—if he could pay for a room for the night?"

When he was sixteen he went to Salt Lake City and worked in a gold mine. Then Jack drifted through Utah, Colorado and Nebraska, living in towns called Cripple Creak and Eureka. And, when he could, he fought for money.

In the ring he called himself Kid Blackie, and as Kid Blackie, he began fighting in the war years of 1915-16. And he won most of those fights, against men with the names of Kid Hancock, Chief Gordon, Joe Lions, Two Round Gillian (Jack got him in one), and Boston Bear Cat, Battling Johnson, Wild Bert Kenney, Fighting Dick Gilbert.

The fighting was tough and the money came tough for Dempsey, and he had no illusions about how far he might go. He was tough, with a mean punch, but he was crude. He had been fighting a long time, and had gotten nowhere. In one ten-round fight in New York, Jack was paid ten dollars.

When he got back to Salt Lake City, which he now considered his hometown, he got a job as a saloon bouncer and fell in love with the piano player, Maxine Cates. They were married in 1916. But there was no money, and Maxine, a woman of dubious reputation, grew fretful. On February 13, 1917, Jack fought Jim Flynn, a far more experienced boxer, and he was knocked out in the first round. He got $500 for the fight, but a bad reputation around Salt Lake, and he moved on. His wife left him.

Finally, Jack's life changed. He met a shrewd thirty-five-year-old manager and promoter, Jack Kearns, and Kearns knew what he had in Dempsey. He immediately began the buildup that would bring them both to the top. After a string of West Coast victories, Dempsey and Kearns moved east, sharing an upper berth to save expenses. This was January 2, 1918, and they arrived in Chicago in the middle of a blizzard, wearing light topcoats and with no money. But the money was to come. During the year 1918, Jack fought twenty-two fights. He lost only one, but he beat all the best heavyweights around—Carl Morris, Billy Miske, Arthur Pelkey, Willy Meehan, Battling Levinsky, Gunboat Smith.

In 1919, after five fights, Jack Kearns steered Dempsey into the ring against Willard and the legend sprang full-blown to life.

It was the Fourth of July, Independence Day, and Toledo, Ohio, was boiling in a heat wave. The temperature in the ring that afternoon—for it was to be an afternoon fight—was 112 degrees.

Jess Willard was feeling the heat even before he stepped into the ring. He was a huge man. He stood 6 feet 6 inches and weighed 250 pounds and he was thirty-six years old and tired. He had won the heavyweight championship four years earlier from Jack Johnson and since then had had only four fights. He was rusty and out of shape.

Jack Dempsey was twenty-four years old and he weighed only 187 pounds, but there was not a trace of fat on his body. He was in perfect condition. He entered the ring wearing a sweater. His face was bearded and wet with perspiration and his eyes glinted dangerously. Side by side it looked like a mismatch. The huge Willard towered over Dempsey, but when you looked into their faces—Willard wore almost a beatific look— you knew, somehow, that size would have no meaning in this fight.

At the beginning, Dempsey moved in cautiously, circling around Willard. The Pottawatomie Giant, as he was called, threw two light lefts and slapped Dempsey into the ropes, and that seemed to ignite Jack. He snapped his left, catching Willard under the heart. Willard winced and dropped his guard momentarily and Dempsey hooked him with a right that exploded on the champion's cheekbone, splattering it into pieces. Willard sank to the floor.

Six more times Willard went down that round. The last time the champion lay unconscious and was saved only by the bell.

In the second round Dempsey seemed content to regain his wind, for the heat was fierce and he knew there was no hurry. The big man was old and sick and his arms were heavy and his legs were weary. Jack could coast a bit.

In the third round Dempsey decided to end it. He leaped from his stool and smashed rights at the champion's mouth, drawing blood. Willard looked helpless.

His face, covered with blood, was cut open in thirteen places and his great stomach heaved as someone wrote, "like the billows on Maumee Bay." Dempsey hooked another left to the face and Willard tottered about the ring. Somehow, though, he managed to stay on his feet, alive.

He stumbled back to his corner at the end of the round, and his seconds had only to look into his face to know that he was through. One of them threw in the towel and 20,000 people roared in tribute to the new champion of the world.

But the tribute was short-lived. The truth was, Jack Dempsey was an unpopular champion. The reason for the unpopularity dated back to the start of World War I. Dempsey, just beginning his career, had gotten a job in an Oakland, California, shipyard. He was accused widely of being a slacker. The government made a test case out of Jack's action, trying to prove that a worker in an essential industry should not be exempt from the draft. Jack had to go to court in 1920. He won the case but it wasn't enough. The stigma stayed with him.

There was another problem with the new champion, too. He was shy and ill at ease in public, with none of the social veneer that the celebrity needs to live in the limelight. "When you're a champion," Dempsey said, "they take your life away from you. They put you on the stage. They put you in nightclubs. They take away the fresh air. They make you live the life of a gentleman of the city. I didn't belong."

In the ring, though, Jack Dempsey belonged. He went on in 1920 to knock out Billy Miske in the third round, and then he knocked out Billy Brennan in the twelfth. Now it was 1921 and Georges Carpentier and the first million-dollar gate.

It was not hard to understand the enormous appeal of this fight. Jack Dempsey, the war "slacker" was to fight Georges Carpentier, the war hero, "the soldier of France," as he was called. Carpentier had education, charm and good looks. He had everything all right, except the right kind of a body to compete with Dempsey.

For one thing he was small; not much more, really, than a light-heavyweight. He had been stopped by Frank Mantell and Billy Papke when he fought as a middleweight. As a heavyweight he had beaten mediocre fighters. But just before Dempsey he had beaten a top heavyweight, Kingfish Levinsky, and he came to New York as David pitted against the Goliath, Dempsey.

It was a shrewd match-up for the greatest promoter of all times, Tex Rickard. Rickard liked nothing better than to cast one fighter as hero, the other as villain. His casting was perfect for this fight and it called for special preparations. Rickard built a stadium in Jersey City, New Jersey, Boyle's Thirty Acres, that seated 50,000. By fight-time, seating capacity had gone to 91,000 and Rickard knew he would have a full house.

The buildup for the fight was intense. Every move both fighters made was duly recorded in the newspapers. Carpentier trained for the fight in secret on a Long Island estate where, said Rickard's press agents, Carpentier was "perfecting a secret punch."

The fight which was held on July 2, 1921 before 91,000 people had a gate of $1,626,580.

Carpentier came into the ring wearing a pearl-gray

robe and thinking, "I don't know where I am. I don't even know if I've come here to fight. I have forgotten everything. I have the feeling that I'm walking on a cotton cloud in a nightmare."

Dempsey had only one thought: annihilation.

But he started off slowly. In the first round he stayed away mostly, measuring Carpentier with a scowl rather than any single blow. In the second, the Frenchman tried to rally. Once he dropped his guard and Dempsey charged and Carpentier countered with a right that sent Jack reeling to the ropes. But the punch also broke Georges' right thumb.

After that, it was just a matter of time. The end came in the fourth round. Dempsey opened with a smash to the body and followed with a volley of lefts and rights to the chin. In close, Dempsey caught Carpentier on the jaw with a right that traveled no more than ten inches. It sent the Frenchman to the canvas. He managed to stumble to his feet at the count of nine and Dempsey was on him like a tiger.

Jack tore a ripping right to George's heart and the Frenchman doubled up in pain. Dempsey followed with a right against the jaw and this time Carpentier toppled over for good.

Not for two years did Dempsey defend his title again. His manager, the wily Kearns, was very cautious about who Dempsey fought. He wanted more big-money gates. He didn't want his man fighting for nothing. On July 4, 1923, Kearns pushed a little far to make a payday for Dempsey. He had Jack fight in a small town named Shelby, Montana, for a guarantee of $300,000.

Jack's opponent was Tommy Gibbons and the

whole promotion was a fiasco. Dempsey and Kearns got their money all right but the promoters went broke on the fight. As a performance, it wasn't much either.

It went fifteen rounds and was the first time Jack had ever had to go that far (he had knocked out every opponent he had beaten until that time). Dempsey tried to knock out the youngster from St. Paul, Minnesota, just as he always tried to knock out every opponent, but he couldn't seem to catch up to him. It was, actually, a fairly close fight. Gibbons won five rounds and the others were close. Near the end, Dempsey was moving in on target but he was unable to put Gibbons down. He finished the fight on the attack while 20,000 fans, who felt they had been suckered, booed and hissed.

Three months later Kearns made everyone forget the Gibbons fight. He put Dempsey in with Luis Firpo —the "Wild Bull of the Pampas." It was—especially one round—one of the most brutal and exciting fights in ring history.

Luis Firpo was an Argentinian with suitable qualifications. His size was one. He stood 6 feet 3 inches and weighed 216 pounds. His experience was another. He had beaten two old Dempsey foes, Bill Brennan and Jess Willard, and he was billed as the undefeated heavyweight champion of South America.

That was enough for the hungry boxing public. An estimated 82,000 fans turned out at New York City's Polo Grounds on September 14, putting $1,188,603 in the till—the second million-dollar gate.

Just before the start, promoter Tex Rickard came into Dempsey's dressing room.

"Will you do me a favor?" Rickard asked. "We got another million-dollar gate out there. If you put this poor dub away with the first punch, all those people out there won't get their money's worth."

"I can't carry this guy," Dempsey said. "He's big and a slugger. He could kill me with one wallop."

"But, Jack, how is he going to hit you? He's slow and moves like an old tub. I hate to think of all them nice millionaires going out of here sore at both of us."

"Nuts to you," said Jack and he turned away.

Rickard needn't have worried. As soon as Dempsey got to mid-ring, Firpo moved in, struck a right and knocked Jack down.

The champion, who had always had tremendous inner resources and a flaming will to take punishment and keep going, bounced up immediately and hammered at Firpo. And now Firpo was down.

Jack ignored the rule about a boxer going to a neutral corner. Instead, he hovered over the referee, waiting for Firpo to get up. The Argentinian rose and then —splat!—was smashed down again.

Seven times in that first round Dempsey knocked Firpo kicking to the canvas, and seven times the courageous Argentinian crawled around and managed to struggle to his feet. And each time he got up he would snarl at Dempsey and rush him. He was truly a wild bull. The blood streamed from his nose and mouth, his eyes were glazed, but he fought on.

The seventh time he rose wearily and then charged Dempsey. He let loose with a jolting right to Jack's jaw, piledriving the champion through the ropes and onto the press table. Jack crushed a typewriter as he fell with both hands and feet in the air, and rolled over on his side.

Now he was in desperate trouble. He was hurt and the official was counting and his title was at stake. Then he received the biggest break of his life. Sportswriters aided Dempsey onto the edge of the ring, helping him to recover from the brutal blow.

He was in the ring at the seven-count. Firpo charged him again. For thirty seconds, he hammered Dempsey with lefts and rights. But Dempsey hung on, clinging to his opponent while absorbing massive punishment.

As he sat in his corner between the first and second rounds, he was still only semiconscious. He couldn't even remember being out of the ring. He came to only when Jack Kearns waved smelling salts under his nose.

"What round was I knocked out in?" he asked Kearns.

"You so and so," said Kearns, "you weren't knocked out. Go out there and box that guy."

He did. In round two, his head clearer, Dempsey went after his man. Firpo came on him with his sledgehammer fists flailing away, but Dempsey fought off the blows and floored Firpo twice.

Then the challenger threw a wild right. Had it landed it might have put Dempsey out for good. It did not land. Dempsey moved under the blow and made a sudden-death rush at Firpo's belly. Then, with the full weight of his body behind the blow, Dempsey delivered a short, crunching left. It landed smack on Firpo's chin. The Argentinian crumpled on the canvas, the blood spurting from his mouth. He was unable to rise at the count of ten. When Firpo was counted out, Dempsey rushed over the help carry the Wild Bull to his corner.

That had to be the artistic highpoint of Jack Dempsey's ring career. For the next three years Jack confined himself to exhibitions while living high. He spent some time in Hollywood squiring actresses. He fell in love with one, Estelle Taylor, and they were married.

Then on September 23, 1926, he made the sixth defense of his heavyweight title. His opponent was a young ex-Marine, Gene Tunney.

It was Dempsey's worst fight. Easy living had done a job on him. Dempsey had toured Europe with his wife, had learned all the social graces, had been lionized by kings and queens and cafe society. His legs were shot and his body was soft and although the killer instinct was still in him, he had been idle too long. The fight went ten rounds and 120,757 fans in Philadelphia—another million-dollar gate—went away happy. Gene Tunney won the decision and the heavyweight championship.

Jack came home that night and his face was a mass of bruises and welts. His wife looked at him and had to fight to hold back tears. "What happened, Dempsey?" she asked.

"Honey," the battered Dempsey said, "I forgot to duck."

But something *had* happened. Out of that fight, the public had begun to change towards Jack Dempsey. Now that he was a loser, now that he was the underdog for the first time in his life, the fight public had switched affections. Now Jack Dempsey was their man.

He came back and in another million-dollar gate, knocked out Jack Sharkey. And that set him up for the rematch with Tunney.

It was held before 104,000 screaming fans at Soldier Field in Chicago and this time the fans screamed for Dempsey. It was a record gate—$2,658,660. This time Dempsey was ready; inasmuch as a thirty-two-year-old man who had been fighting almost all his life could be termed ready.

The first six rounds Tunney boxed and Jack struggled. In the third he hit Gene below the heart and Tunney was hurt. But mostly in those rounds, Tunney, the educated boxer, was piling up the points against Dempsey, the willing but aged aggressor. Tunney simply would not fight Dempsey's kind of fight. He would out-box Dempsey, wear him down. That was the strategy.

At one point, Dempsey, disgusted because he couldn't close with Tunney, made a dramatic pawing gesture with his gloves. "Come on. Come on and fight!" he taunted. But Tunney ignored Dempsey.

Then in the seventh round, feeling his reserves going, and, knowing that he was tiring and losing the fight, Jack decided to make one last desperate stand. Suddenly, he plunged in on Tunney. He caught Gene with a left flush on the jaw and Tunney wavered.

Now he was on top of him. Now Dempsey was the Manassa Mauler of old, fighting with a snarl and a curse. He hit Tunney with six straight lefts and rights and Tunney fell to the ropes. Slowly, the champion collapsed to a sitting position, dazed and momentariarily lacking his senses. It was the first time he had ever been floored.

Dempsey stood over him. He refused to back away. The referee, Dave Barry, grabbed Jack and pointed to a neutral corner. "Go over there," he shouted.

"I stay," said Jack. Later he explained that he had fought too many fights where you stood over your opponent and waited until he got up and then smashed him down again. That was his code of the ring. That was always Jack Dempsey's code.

"Go over there!" commanded Barry again.

Finally, Dempsey moved. But about four seconds had elapsed in which the referee refused to count.

Gene Tunney took advantage of those extra seconds. He waited until the referee counted nine—which made it thirteen seconds all told—and then he got up and Dempsey's last chance was over. The "long count" had saved the champion.

Tunney put Dempsey down in the eighth but Jack got up, dazed and tired, his legs trembling. He got up and moved in. He stayed two more rounds with Tunney. Gene knocked him down again in the tenth, but Dempsey lasted. Tunney retained his championship. Dempsey recovered his dignity.

It should have been the end of an era, but it wasn't. For Jack Dempsey it was really another beginning.

In 1931 when he was thirty-six years old, he emerged from retirement. He engaged in seventy-two bouts, and appeared mostly in exhibitions until about 1940. Everywhere he went the fans who once booed and hissed him, now stood up and cheered him. They crowded his dressing room and told him he was the greatest fighter who ever lived.

Dempsey divorced his actress wife and married Hannah Williams, a singer. They had two daughters, Joan and Barbara, and Jack became a devoted father. When the girls were small, he used to wheel them in their carriage through Central Park. When Dempsey and Hannah were divorced a few years later he was given custody of the children.

He was almost fifty years old, when he decided he wanted to take part in World War II. He went into the Coast Guard, instructed in physical training and refereed fights on boats shuttling GIs to Europe and the Pacific. On the final big assault of World War II, Okinawa, Jack Dempsey was in one of the landing crafts headed toward the beach that was soon to be bloodied and strewn with American corpses. He did his best to cheer up the boys, hollering, "See ya on Broadway."

And so today, as he sits in his restaurant and shakes hands with his admirers, he is happy in the twilight of his life, and content with the public image. The late John Lardner, writing of the public image, pictured Jack as "the two-handed fighter who stormed forward, a flame of red fire in the ring, strong, native, affable, easy of speech, close to the people in word, deed and feeling."

The flame of red fire has not yet been extinguished and Jack Dempsey remains, still, close to the people.

Jim Brown

SOMETIME AGO I was asked to testify at the trial of a famous professional athlete who was being sued by the bureau of internal revenue for not declaring certain gifts given to him as awards during the course of a season. The contention of the athlete, and of his lawyer, was that the awards were earned by extraordinary performance—by the science and artistry of the athlete on the playing field. There is an exemption in the internal revenue code for artists, writers and the like who may receive awards because of their work. Thus, for instance, the Nobel prize is awarded tax free.

"Do you regard sports such as baseball and football and boxing as artistic endeavors?" the athlete's lawyer asked me. I answered that I did.

"What is an artist in sports?" asked the lawyer.

"An artist in sports," I said, "is the gifted athletic performer who creates, who does wonderful things that the ordinary person cannot do, who does them through instinct, through sheer natural instinct backed by years of training and experience."

Here, the judge interrupted. He looked at me sternly and said, "If you had to name one person in sports today who typifies the artist-athlete, could you name one?"

"Yes, your Honor," I said.

"Who would that be?"

"Jim Brown."

And so it was. Jim Brown was the first sports artist of the television age. He was there week after week during the football season, year after year, for all to see. He was the first artist developed and nurtured through the medium of television. When you tuned into a Cleveland Browns' game, you were seldom disappointed by Jim Brown. He was always demonstrating his artistry.

Such a demonstration took place late in the 1965 season when the Browns were driving for an Eastern Conference title in the National Football League. The Browns were playing the Dallas Cowboys and the game was being nationally televised. In the first period, the score tied 3-3, Cleveland had the ball on the Cowboys' three yard line. It was third down and everyone knew what the call would be. The 76,250 fans in the Cotton Bowl knew what the call would be. The Dallas Cowboys certainly knew what the call would be.

The Browns broke huddle and Jim Brown lined up to the rear and just to the right of the quarterback, Frank Ryan. At the snap from center, Brown started in motion left and Ryan tucked the ball into the fullback's chest. Jim was sweeping wide left and the Cowboys were ready. The Dallas linebackers came up to meet him, the defensive back pinched in. Someone on the Cleveland team missed a block. Brown was hemmed in near the sidelines, with three men converging in on him. He should have been stopped at the line, should at least have been knocked forward. Certainly, there was no way for Jim Brown to move forward. But he is an artist, remember?

He slipped one tackle from the right with a hip feint. He took the full brunt of a thigh-high tackle from the left. He shuddered, lost his footing, and began sliding to the ground. Only, in mid-air, the slide seemed to be arrested. Somehow, Jim Brown had regained his balance, though now it was the precarious balance of a drunk reeling down the street. Somehow, he was groping his way forward, clawing, crawling, sprawling his way toward the end zone, with his body stretched parallel and just a few inches above the ground. He seemed to be going in on his hands and knees, but his knee never touched the ground. He flopped in the end zone and then allowed himself the luxury of collapsing. It was an impossible run but Jim

Brown had made it. Jim Brown, the artist, had done it. Nobody else could have.

That one went only three yards, nothing for Jim Brown who regularly ripped off sixty-yard runs from scrimmage who, in his nine-year professional career, rushed for 12,312 yards in the National Football League, and scored 126 touchdowns, the career high in the NFL. The artist at work.

Almost from the beginning of his pro career, he was described as an artist. In 1962, Myron Cope wrote of Brown, "As he carries the ball, churning, veering, shifting speeds, the game of football becomes an art form which awes even the most insensitive of spectators."

An art form. "If the NFL exists another 2,000 years," said Brown's teammate, Dick Modzelewski, "there won't be a fullback as good as him." And Dick's brother, Ed, who was the Cleveland fullback before Jim Brown, echoed the statement. "I'll tell you," Big Mo once said, "I feel like the guy who played behind Babe Ruth."

Jim Brown is the Babe Ruth of football, only more so. Ruth's competitors were strong, respected. Babe Ruth hit more home runs than any man alive, but some men gave him a chase. Jim Brown—he sits alone on a pedestal. His 12,312 yards in just nine pro years is far and away the best in the NFL. His nearest competitor, Joe Perry, ran for 8,578 yards in a fourteen-year career. Jim Brown sits alone—indestructible, superhuman.

This was perhaps the most awesome aspect of Jim Brown's career. He played a game that is dedicated to violence. People hurt people in pro football. Yet Jim

Brown never got hurt, never really got hurt. Or, if he was hurt, he refused to let his opponents know it. He played. Paul Hornung, not a bad running back himself, wrote about Brown in his book, *Football and the Single Man*. "As many times as you carry the ball," Hornung wrote, "you've got to get hurt. I mean you have guys 285 pounds who get hurt. But Jimmy Brown never gets hurt. He's got 230 pounds on him and not an ounce of fat on him, and he's built like a llama and he runs like a llama—swoosh, he takes off and he's gone." Frank Gifford, another fair running back in his day, put it even more succinctly.

"He says he isn't Superman," Gifford said. "What he means is that Superman isn't Jimmy Brown."

He *was* Superman and he looked the part. At his peak he stood 6 feet 2 inches and weighed 228 pounds. His forty-seven inch chest tapered like an hourglass to a thirty-two inch waist, and his handsome mahogany-colored face was like that of a Greek god. He has a wife and three boys and earned $60,000 a year playing football, and maybe a third more on the outside. He had everything, including that magic known as presence.

One day, shortly after the 1965 football season, Cassius Clay, the heavyweight boxing champion of the world, was entertaining some people in his hotel room in New York City. Now Cassius Clay is no midget. He is 6 foot 3 inches and weighs 210 pounds. He is broad-shouldered and muscular, the picture of what a heavyweight champion should look like. Cassius was prancing around the room when there was an unexpected knock on the door. It was Jim Brown and as he stepped into the room, Cassius Clay suddenly looked *small*. He sensed it too. He rushed over to Brown, who stood there stolidly in an immaculate, closely fitted black suit. He rushed over to Brown and put his arms around him and started pummeling him lightly around the shoulders, and then slipped down and tried tackling Jim around his custom-styled trousers, which have to be altered to allow for bulging thigh and calf muscles. "He's my man!" Cassius screamed. What he really was saying was, "He's my master."

He *was* Clay's master, and a spectator got the feeling that had Brown chosen to be a boxer instead of a football player, he could have taken Cassius Clay out with one punch. But Jim Brown chose pro football and that was quite enough. Jim Brown's career record should be put into a space capsule for future civilizations to ponder. It is a relic of our civilization, a fragment that deserves to be saved.

Through his nine seasons in the NFL, Jim Brown led the league in rushing eight times. In seven of those seasons he rushed for over two hundred yards in a game. He holds all the meaningful rushing records —most attempts in a season and a lifetime, most yards gained in a season and lifetime, most yards gained in a game (237, which he did twice), most games 100 or more yards rushing in a lifetime, most touchdowns in a lifetime. But Jim Brown does not like to mull over statistics. "They are very cold—cut and dried," he said. "They don't really tell the story."

The story, rather, is told through the man and the tracks he made from his birthplace, St. Simon's Island in Georgia on February 17, 1936, to Cleveland. Everywhere he went, the tracks were clearly defined.

He was christened James Nathaniel Brown. "My mother was Theresa Brown, hard-working domestic,"

Jimmy writes in his autobiography, *Off My Chest,* and my father was Swinton (Sweet Sue) Brown, gambling man."

His mother and father separated shortly after Jim was born, and the first nine years of his life he was raised by his grandmother. Then his mother, who was working for a well-to-do family in the wealthy New York suburb of Great Neck, sent for Jimmy. Jimmy and his mother lived in a small one-bedroom apartment off the kitchen and Jimmy commuted to school in Manhasset, Long Island, several miles from Great Neck.

In Georgia, Jimmy had never played football. The first game he saw in Manhasset was played on a corner lot that had been picked clean of rocks and broken glass. But he was a natural at every sport from the beginning. At Plandome Road Junior High School, Jimmy began to play basketball, lacrosse and six-man football. And his coach, Jay Stranahan, told him, "Jimmy, you have tremendous natural ability. Don't waste it."

Jim Brown wasn't about to waste it. He went on to high school in Manhasset and became a star in everything he tried—track and field, basketball, baseball, lacrosse and football. The big influence in his life then was the Manhasset High School football coach, Ed Walsh. "He was my idea of a saint," Brown wrote in his autobiography. "I am convinced that Ed Walsh had not one iota of bigotry in him." Ed Walsh taught Brown the fundamentals of football and he taught Brown character. Once when Brown was doing poorly in his academic work, Walsh had a long talk with Jim.

"Jimmy," Walsh said, "you can be a professional football player. But you've got to go to college first, and you won't go to college unless you start taking your studies seriously."

Brown started to take his studies seriously, started to take everything seriously. He made the first team in football as a thirteen-year-old freshman. As a junior he averaged 15.1 yards a carry. As a 6-foot 1-inch, 200-pound senior halfback, he averaged 14.9 yards a carry. In his four years of football, his high school team lost only two games, one by a touchdown, one by a point. "It's hard to believe," he recalled, "but I made better moves and cuts in high school than I've made in college and pro ball." It surely is hard to believe.

And he excelled in other sports, too. He was a star in lacrosse. In basketball, he set a Long Island high school record by scoring fifty-five points in a game. He averaged thirty-eight points as a senior. By that time, the colleges were flocking around him. He had forty-five college offers. With the help of a local attorney and Syracuse alumnus, Kenneth Molloy, Jim chose Syracuse.

At first, it seemed a poor choice to Jim. Everything seemed to go wrong his freshman year. For one, he was the only Negro on the football team. For another, the coaches thought he would be better as an end rather than a halfback. He didn't get to start a game until the seventh game of his sophomore year against Colgate. In the previous game against Cornell, Jim had come in as a substitute left halfback and gained 151 yards, including a fifty-four yard touchdown run. Now he was a starter. He made the most of it. He scored touchdowns on runs of forty-one and seventeen yards. He started every game from then on.

He was an All-American as a junior and a senior. In his junior year one rival coach said, "He's the greatest back I've seen since Glenn Davis." Another coach, one week later, said, "He's the most powerful runner to come along since Doc Blanchard." Nobody had ever before compared one man to *both of the great Army stars of the mid-1940's.*

As a senior, Jim set a one-year Syracuse record, running for 986 yards in eight games. He averaged 6.2 yards a carry. He kicked off and kicked extra points. Against Colgate, in Syracuse's final game of the 1956 season, with a Bowl bid hinging on how well the Orange showed, Jim scored forty-three points on six touchdowns and seven conversions, and he rushed for 197 yards.

That game earned Syracuse an invitation to the Cotton Bowl in 1957 and again Brown was magnificent against a much stronger Texas Christian squad. Syracuse lost by one point, 28-27, but it was hardly Jim Brown's fault. He scored twenty-one of the twenty-seven points. He ran back three kickoffs for ninety-six yards. He completed two of the three passes for twenty yards.

And still he had time for other sports. He played basketball. He was an All-American in lacrosse and tied for the national scoring championship as a senior "I've never seen a better lacrosse player," said the president of the U.S. Intercollegiate Lacrosse Association.

His last performance as a Syracuse athlete was a memorable one. It came in the spring when Syracuse scheduled a lacrosse and track doubleheader against Army. There were 7,500 people in the stands and they had come out to see Jim Brown. And they saw. Jim scored thirteen points in the track meet, then changed uniforms and led the lacrosse team to victory.

Whatever Jim Brown tried, it seemed, Jim Brown excelled. If he chose he could have made the Olympic track team in the decathlon event (he actually finished fifth in the national decathlon trials, without adequate preparation). "He could have been national college heavyweight champion," said the boxing coach at Syracuse. He could have played professional baseball, too.

But professional football would be his game, his career. The Cleveland Browns drafted him No. 1 at the end of the 1956 season and Cleveland coach Paul Brown was full of hope for Jim Brown. "We hope he will be the next Marion Motley," Paul Brown said, hopefully. "He has a lot of the same attributes as Motley—size, speed, good running sense, and power. He should get the extra yard and he should hurt opponents when they tackle him, just like Motley did."

He hurt opponents all right. Right away, Jim Brown showed his coach. He came back from the college All-Star game and started the Brown's second exhibition game against the Pittsburgh Steelers. He played most of the game. On a draw play he broke through the middle of the Pittsburgh line, then shifted into high and raced through the converging defensive backs for forty-eight yards and a touchdown. When he came back to the bench, Paul Brown shook his hand. The usually dour Brown had a small smile on his face.

"Well, you're my fullback," he said. And Jim Brown's face lighted up.

But Ed Modzelewski was the starting fullback and Jim had to beat him out. Big Mo had a lot of friends on the team and they made it tough for Brown in scrimmages. They would try to hit him a little harder than they normally would, because Mo was their boy. But Jim kept busting out of their arms, kept going down and coming up for more and, gradually, the veteran players began to gain respect for No. 32.

Jim started the season and was a revelation from the beginning. On November 24, 1957, he really showed what he could do.

The temperature was 35 degrees at Cleveland Stadium and a crowd of 65,407 were huddled in a biting wind to see the Browns play the tough Los Angeles Rams. These were the Rams of Elroy "Crazy Legs" Hirsch, of Norm Van Brocklin, of Jon Arnett, of Tommy Wilson who, a year earlier, had set a rushing record for one game, 223 yards.

Early in the game, Jim Brown scored the Browns' first touchdown. Now, midway in the first quarter, Cleveland had the ball on their own thirty-one. The call was for a fullback draw. Two Ram linebackers, Dick Daugherty and Larry Morris, blitzed and hit Jim from both sides as he was handed the ball by quarterback Milt Plum. Daughtery cracked so hard his helmet flew off at impact. Jim staggered in and out of Morris' arms. Then he bounced free and, suddenly, he was alone. The last five yards of his sixty-nine yard touchdown run, he carried the safetyman with him into the end zone.

The Browns couldn't hold the 14-0 lead and at half time the Rams led 21-17. Then, in the third period, Brown fumbled on his twenty-nine, the loose ball was picked up by a Ram and run in. Now the Rams led 28-17. Now Jim Brown had to make up for that error.

He did, as soon as Cleveland got the ball. Jim raced

thirty-three yards to the Rams' ten, then took the ball in. Moments later Van Brocklin was spilled on the seven and Jim rammed over from the one. That made it Browns, 31, Rams 28.

In the last quarter Jim ran another forty-six yards to bring the ball to the five and set up another touchdown. The final score was Browns 45, Rams 31. Jim Brown had scored four touchdowns and, in thirty-one carries, racked up 237 yards—a new National Football League record.

He won his first rushing championship that year, with 942 yards in 202 attempts, and his nine touchdowns were tops among runners. Jim Brown was the overwhelming choice as NFL rookie-of-the-year.

The next year he was even better, running for 1,527 yards, a 5.9 average; he also scored seventeen touchdowns. In 1959 he ran for another 1,329 yards; in 1960, 1,257 yards; in 1961, 1,408 yards. He seemed to be doing it all and yet he wasn't completely happy, wasn't completely fulfilled. Something was wrong.

The problem for Jim Brown was the coach. Paul Brown was a brilliant football technician. In twelve years, from 1946 through 1957, the Browns had won eleven divisional championships in the All-American Conference and then the NFL. But the Browns were unable to win an Eastern Conference title after that and some of the players felt that the coach hadn't kept up with the times, hadn't kept abreast of the changes that were taking place in the game.

In addition, Brown was a tough, demanding coach who treated his players like robots. He called every play himself. He refused to let his fullback deviate at all from the script. If Jim Brown were told to run through right guard, that's where he had to run. In a sense, Paul Brown was shackling Jim Brown's creativity. Jim was a workhorse for his coach—in 1961 he carried the ball 305 times—but he had to carry the ball as Paul Brown directed him. "I used to run from guard to guard," Brown once said, and he was not being facetious.

In 1962 Jim hurt his left wrist early in the season and it hampered him most of the year. He normally carried the ball with his left arm and used his right arm to ward off tacklers. Now he had to protect his injury and make ground at the same time. Paul Brown began to needle him when he fumbled. Jim resented this very much.

That year an unhappy Brown rushed for "only" 996 yards and for the first time since his entry into the league, he lost the rushing title (to Jim Taylor). But at the end of the season the new Browns' owner, Arthur Modell, made a drastic move. He kicked Paul Brown upstairs as a vice president and named a Brown assistant, Blanton Collier, as head coach.

Jim Brown and most of the other Cleveland players were very happy at the change. Collier had been backfield coach of the Browns and Jim Brown admired Collier, and the admiration was mutual. Collier opened up the offense for Brown. He put in new sweep plays, pitchouts and the like, so that Jim could run to the outside as well as the inside, so that he could utilize his speed and shiftiness as well as his power. And he gave Jim his head, allowing him the opportunity to improvise if the situation called for it. How did he improvise? He once explained.

"You take the ball at full speed," he said. "You

watch your block develop, then you decide on just how fast to go. You stay with the blocker and when he starts to make contact, you shoot by him. A lot of times you hit a pileup. And because there are a lot of guys around, the defense thinks they have you. So they relax. Then with movement, no specific kind, but just movement of your body and legs, you find yourself getting free. In other words, you never feel that you're caught until you're down."

That is Jim Brown's philosophy of running with the football; that is his art, and he has never wavered from it. But now he had the freedom to express his art as he never had before.

In 1963, in game after game, the twenty-seven-year-old fullback was expressing himself fully. In an early season game against Dallas in the Cotton Bowl, in 100-degree temperature, Jim ran for 232 yards. On one seventy-one yard touchdown run he was stopped after a three-yard gain when he hit a stack of Cowboys. But he rolled off with second effort. Someone grabbed his shirt. He jerked away; seventy-one yards. Later he split the left guard and tackle and ran sixty-two yards. Afterwards, Dallas coach Tom Landry could only shake his head. "I have no doubt that Brown is football's finest runner of all time," said Landry. "Why is he such a great runner? Well, it's all in leg drive. Brown's tremendous. He won't go down until you put him down. He is very fast and has great balance."

New York Giant coach Allie Sherman saw another view of Brown that same year, in an October game in New York. Cleveland came into Yankee Stadium unbeaten. The Giants, defending Eastern Conference champions, now had to stop them. And to stop them, they had to stop Jim Brown.

No chance.

He played like a man trying to shuck off demons. He kept ripping off gains of seven, eight yards, shedding tacklers like peanuts shells, straightarming defenders and leaving them impotent on the ground. With the ball on the Giants' five, he picked up four yards, five Giant tacklers clinging to him all the way. On the next play he made the touchdown by hurling himself bodily into the air.

But despite Brown the Giants still led, 17-14, at the start of the third period. Now Jim Brown really took charge. On Cleveland's first play of the second half, he caught a screen pass from Frank Ryan, turned on the gas and went seventy-two yards for the touchdown. At the end, Giant defender Erich Barnes, a ten-flat sprinter, could only look on in astonishment. But Jim was not finished.

Midway in the third period, the ball rested on the Giant thirty-two. Frank Ryan called "Option Seven left." Jim took the pitchout and slid toward his left. He hit through left tackle and found his left tackle blocking inside. He drove outside the hole to the twenty-five where he was met by a wall of blue uniforms. They rushed in at him.

He cut sharply to his right, pirouetting nearly 180 degrees in a flash of grace. He ran parallel to the line of scrimmage, picking up blockers. He moved effortlessly behind his blockers and just glided free into the end zone. "We had him, we had him," moaned defensive captain Andy Robustelli. "We had him and still we couldn't get him."

It went that way all afternoon. He would pound through the Giant line, then pick himself up as if he had just drawn his last breath. But that was Jim

Brown's way. He always rose from the turf slowly, tiptoeing back to the huddle as if the ground were just too much of a burden for his feet. "It keeps the defense unaware of my physical condition," Jim once explained. "Maybe I've had the wind knocked out of me. But nobody really knows. And I'm saving my energy for the next play."

The Giants had had the wind knocked out of them and the Browns won the game 35-24. Afterwards, Allie Sherman tried to explain this phenomenon named Brown. "Watch his feet," Allie said, re-running the films of the game. "He's like a scatback. He's like a big express train going around there and he cuts like a scatback. He gets them the yards. Four yards of pop will keep you in any running game and, heck, he falls down for four yards."

He was "popping" all of 1963. It was his greatest season. He set a new single-season rushing record, 1,863 yards. His 6.4 per carry average was the highest of his career. He scored twelve touchdowns. But the Browns were unable to win the Eastern Conference and Jim Brown still had that one goal left—to play with a championship team.

It came in 1964 and again Jim Brown led the way. He ran for 1,446 yards. His 5.2 average was the best in the league. He was running with his usual devastating mixture of scatback speed and fullback power. He would hit tacklers, plow through them like the Twentieth Century Limited running through the night, turn on the juice and be gone.

In 1964 the Browns won the Eastern Conference title and now had only to beat the Baltimore Colts for the NFL championship. But the Colts, with John

Unitas, with Lenny Moore, with Raymond Berry, were strong favorites to beat the Browns.

Form took a licking at Cleveland's Municipal Stadium. In bitter cold, with flurries of snow whipping over the field, it was the Browns who turned it on, not the Colts. Frank Ryan threw three touchdown passes. Gary Collins caught three passes. And Jim Brown, as always, bore the running burden.

The first half was scoreless but Lou Groza kicked a field goal early in the third quarter, and then Brown broke the game apart.

With the ball on the Cleveland thirty-two, quarterback Ryan brought the team out in a double wing, with halfback Ernie Green set as a flanker to the left. The only man behind Ryan in the backfield was Jim Brown.

The play was a quick pitchout to Brown swinging to his left. Jim swept around the pinched-in Colts' linebacker with three blockers in front of him. The defensive halfback was too far back to come up and stop him. Brown ran for forty-six yards before he was stopped; ran to the Baltimore eighteen-yard line. The Browns were on their way. All in all, in Cleveland's 27-0 upset victory, Brown carried twenty-seven times for 114 yards. It was his most satisfying victory.

If he was satisfied, his teammates were absolutely delirious. Defensive end Paul Wiggin said, "Jim Brown is our team's No. 1 source of inspiration." Blanton Collier was even more emphatic. "He is," said Collier, "the best running back in the history of professional football."

And history's best running back just kept on going. He had another brilliant season in 1965—twenty-one touchdowns, 1,544 yards gained rushing. He could not be stopped.

Unfortunately, the Browns were stopped in 1965. They did win the Eastern Conference title for the second year in a row but Green Bay beat the Browns in the championship game in Green Bay. The weather was snowy and the field was soggy and treacherous and Jim was just unable to run with his usual force.

And that was it, that was the end of one of the most remarkable football careers of all time. Shortly before the opening of training camp in the summer of 1966, Jimmy Brown announced his retirement from football. He had decided to devote himself to the gentler world of make-believe, to work hard at becoming a movie actor, and also to spend more time promoting civil rights causes.

"I quit with regret," he said, "but no sorrow. You should get out at the top." Jim Brown, the artist, did just that. And professional football is still not quite the same.

Ty Cobb

TODAY, the watchword in baseball is—speed. Maury Wills stole 102 bases in 1962 and baseball hasn't been the same since. No longer is the home run hitter quite the force in baseball he once was. No longer is power the name of the game. The name of the game today is speed.

It was that way once before. It was that way when Ty Cobb was playing baseball, when speed meant Ty Cobb; indeed, when baseball meant Ty Cobb.

For Ty Cobb was more than speed. He was also the greatest hitter who ever lived. His lifetime batting average of .363 surely will never be topped, nor his feat of leading the American League in batting for nine straight years and twelve years in all. He was hitting, and fielding, and throwing. He did it all, but when one thinks of Ty Cobb today, of what he symbolized, one thinks first of speed. Speed, above all.

He was not the fastest man ever to play baseball, not even the fastest man of his time. It was the way he utilized his speed, and his intelligence, and his cunning, and his go-for-broke approach. On the bases there was no one, ever, like Ty Cobb. He ran the bases with reckless abandon, with headlong excitement. He ran with sharpened spikes flying high and let no man get in his way or he would be left bleeding and cut to shreds.

Speed and terror. Those were his devices on the bases. A pitcher could get rid of Babe Ruth by walking him, but there was no answer for Ty Cobb. Putting Ty Cobb on base was like playing Russian roulette. The man had developed the hook and fadeaway slide. The man could score from first on a single. The man could go from first to third on a sacrifice bunt. The man could score from second on infield outs and sacrifice flies. The man could get himself trapped between bases, sometimes on purpose, and still slide in safe.

There was one game when Cobb was on second and the hitter lifted a fly to left field. The ball was caught and Cobb took off—took off from second base even though the ball had been taken in shallow left field. The left fielder threw and everyone waited for the patented Cobb slide and then the umpire's call. But Ty Cobb wasn't sliding. He was coming into third at a 45-degree angle, touching the base with a toe and, without changing pace, heading for home. And sliding in safely.

Cobb was the thinking man's base-runner. He had figured that the third-baseman would be expecting the slide, and that since he would have his back to the plate he would have to turn and cross his legs to throw. And by then it would be too late to catch Cobb. And it was.

Another time he similarly victimized the best fielding first-baseman in baseball, Hal Chase. Chase used an artful weapon on runners. When a man was on second base and the ball was hit to the infield, Chase's habit was to make the putout and then fire the ball to third, catching the runner rounding the bag. It was a pattern that had succeeded for years for Chase. But one year Cobb made the pattern work for him.

Game after game, when the Detroit Tigers played Chase's New York Highlanders, Cobb would move from second to third on an infield grounder, round the bag, and dive back, always just ahead of Chase's throw. This procedure went on for most of the season. And then, one day, Cobb saw his chance.

He was on second when the batter hit a grounder to second base. Cobb took off for third and rounded the bag as Hal Chase made the putout and threw to third. The third-baseman swung around to tag Cobb as he slid back. Only Ty wasn't sliding back. He was scoring.

It was always planning with Cobb. Over and over again, he said to himself, "Here's what I do in this situation." And he went ahead and did it.

Intelligence. But it was more than intelligence with Ty Cobb. In the annals of baseball there simply was no competitor like Cobb. He excelled because he was driven to it by something inside of him. Excellence in baseball was a necessity of life for Ty Cobb. People who got to know him later in life claim that he was a paranoid personality; that he was cruel, even murderous, and that his urge to excel came from deep psychological wounds imbedded deep inside him at the beginning of his baseball career after his father was accidentally shot to death by his mother.

Maybe so, but wherever that urge came from, it was there—and that was why he was the man of unparalleled grace at bat and unparalleled beauty on the bases, and the reason he was the most flaming competitor ever.

He was born on December 18, 1886, in Royston, Georgia. Ty's mother, Amanda Chitwood Cobb, was a gentle and good woman. His father, W.H. Cobb, was at one time superintendent of county schools and also a state senator. And everyone addressed him as "Senator." The father was always a profound influence on Ty. "My father," Ty Cobb once said, "was the greatest man I ever knew. He was a scholar, state senator, editor and philosopher. I worshipped him. He was the only man who ever made me do his bidding."

Ty started playing baseball for his church team, and from the first he was a natural. Before he was fifteen he was the town's best hitter, and base-runner, and his team's regular shortstop.

But Senator Cobb, who was wealthy and aristocratic, felt that baseball was nothing more than a frivolous diversion. He wanted his son to become a lawyer. He would make Ty go down to the local judge's office and read about the law. But Ty preferred looking out the window. He preferred baseball.

It was inevitable that the two should clash head on because the son was growing to be as strong-willed as the father. When he was seventeen he started writing letters to various ballclubs in the South Atlantic League asking for a tryout. When his father heard about it, he was furious. "Baseball is a hoodlum's game," he told his son.

"Baseball is *my* game," Cobb answered. "I want to play it."

They argued through most of one night and, finally, the elder Cobb gave in. Ty set out for Augusta, for a tryout with the Augusta, Georgia, team with his father's parting words ringing in his ears: "Stop being so bullheaded. Learn to take orders. If you don't you'll be fired before the season is out."

But Ty couldn't take orders. He played thirty-seven games for Augusta, batted .237, and did things *his* way. In one game he hit a home run and a double. The home run was hit after he had been told to bunt. He was sent down to Anniston and did better, batting .370 in twenty-two games.

He was, at that time, a bit of a freak as a batter. He held his hands six inches apart on the bat, not together as everyone else did. Once he explained why. "When I was a kid, I played with boys who were bigger than me. I had to use their bats, and they were too heavy. I found the best way to manage the bat was to put one hand down at the end and the other up six inches to get better leverage. Then I could get the bat around on the ball."

He began to get the bat around on the ball, all right. In 1905 he went back to Augusta determined to make good. He began to study pitchers "to see what they had that could hurt me," he once said, "and to figure out how to stop them."

He figured it out. He hit .326 that year. But it was also the year of the great tragedy in his life.

One night in August of 1905, his father had come home, unexpectedly, late at night. He had to climb through the bedroom window because he had forgotten his key. His wife kept a shotgun beside her bed, in case of intruders. She saw the figure coming through the window. She shot and killed the man, her husband.

Years later Cobb said, "I didn't get over that. I've never gotten over that."

A few days after his father's death, Ty was notified that he had been purchased by the Detroit Tigers. "In my grief," Cobb wrote in his autobiography, "it didn't matter much."

But something indeed had happened to the eighteen-year-old. His will had hardened. It was as though he had put a tough, protective casing around his body. Nobody would ever penetrate that hard shell. Ty Cobb, from that time on, would be his own man, go his own way—and to heck with the world.

He was bought by the Tigers, for $750, and he batted just .240 for the balance of that season. But in 1906 he succeeded in every way. By the end of the season he was the team's regular center fielder, he batted .320, with twenty-three stolen bases. And he earned one other distinction. He made an enemy of every player on the team.

He was a rookie of course and rookies, especially in those days, were treated like slaves. But it was more than being a rookie with Ty Cobb. There was something about him. Early that year his roommate, Nap Rucker, who later went on to fame with the Brooklyn Dodgers, got in the shower ahead of Cobb. When Rucker emerged from the bathroom, Cobb was livid.

"I take my shower first," he said savagely.

"What's the matter with you?" the dumbfounded Rucker said. "You gone crazy? Just 'cause I got to the shower first today?"

Cobb spoke in slow, measured tones. "Please try to understand," he said, "I've got to be first no matter what it is."

Years later, Cobb told about that rookie year. "I hated my teammates as much as they hated me. Later, I was grateful for what they did for me by driving me off by myself. I ate alone, roomed alone, and walked alone. I didn't have much time to do anything but walk, which helped to keep my legs in shape. And walking or sitting, I had plenty of time to think. I thought of how to hit pitchers, how to play the hitters, and how to run the bases."

In 1907, twenty-one years old, a sleek, 175-pound 6-footer, with tight lips, a piercing jaw, and crafty ice eyes, Ty Cobb put it all together. He won his first batting title with a .350 average on 212 hits. He also led the American League in stolen bases with forty-nine, runs batted in, 116, and total bases—and the Tigers won the American League pennant.

Then he became a holdout. He demanded $5,000 a year. Detroit owner Frank Navin refused. Cobb sat home, sat out spring training. Finally, Navin offered $4,500. Cobb settled for it.

He was almost as much a genius as a businessman as he was a ballplayer. Before his career ended he was earning $40,000 a year, an astounding salary in those days, more than anyone had ever earned in baseball, more than anyone would earn until Babe Ruth came along.

And he was careful with his money. He invested it in automobile companies and in a soft drink called Coca-Cola. Later, these investments would make him a millionaire. His philosophy about baseball and money was simple. "I wanted to give my best to the game," he said, "but I wanted all the money I could get in return. I didn't want to be considered just another muscle-worker."

He was not just another muscle-worker. He won two more batting titles in 1908 and 1909, as the Tigers were winning two more pennants. In 1909 he not only hit .377, he also stole seventy-six bases. In his fourth year as a regular major-leaguer, he had established himself as the most feared base-runner in baseball.

Then, in 1910, his baserunning led to one of the most controversial incidents of his life.

It was a tense, late-season game against the Philadelphia Athletics. The Athletics were fighting for a pennant and their leader was third-baseman Frank "Home Run" Baker. In a late inning the Tigers started a rally. Cobb was on first when the next batter singled. Ty rounded second, kept going and flashed into third, his spikes riding high. When the dust cleared, Baker was walking off the field, his arm dripping blood.

There was an immediate uproar. The Athletics charged that Cobb had deliberately spiked Baker. Cobb denied it. The fans got into the act by mailing threatening letters to Cobb. One stated that Cobb would be shot from one of the buildings outside the park. Ban Johnson, president of the American League, investigated. He would have liked to have disciplined Cobb and made an example of him for playing "dirty" baseball. But a photographer had taken a picture of the incident. The photo showed that Cobb, instead of diving at Baker, had slid in from the other side of the base to avoid the fielder.

"Don't anyone ever tell you I was a dirty ball-player," Cobb said years later. "When you're out on those paths, you've got to protect yourself. The base-paths belonged to me, the runner. The rules gave me that right. I always went into a bag full speed, feet first. I had sharp spikes on my shoes. If the baseman stood where he had no business to and got hurt, it was his fault."

That was the defiant challenge Cobb hurled at

baseball. He would hand out punishment in his own righteousness. But he was not afraid to take it, either. The wild, reckless way he played ball left scars on Cobb, too. "I saw him in one series where each leg was a mass of raw flesh," Grantland Rice once wrote. "He had a temperature of 103. The doctor had ordered him to bed for a three-day rest. That afternoon he got three hits and stole three bases, sliding into second and third on sore, battered flesh."

Another time he goaded a teammate, Charlie "Dutch" Schmidt, into a fight. Schmidt weighed 210 pounds and had once boxed Jack Johnson but Cobb took one look at him and screamed,, "You're yellow! You're a skunk with yellow stripes and you stink! You're just a big muscle-bound ape and you haven't got an ounce of guts in your body."

That was too much for the easygoing Schmidt. He weighed into Cobb and mauled him. He hit Cobb in the body and on the face. He sent Cobb reeling from wall to wall. He broke Cobb's nose. He asked Cobb if he had had enough and when Cobb said no, he continued to batter him. Ty kept coming up for more—he simply would not give up—and, finally, his teammates had to drag Schmidt off the bleeding, battered but still defiant Cobb.

But between fights, and between spikings, and between feuds with teammates, Ty Cobb played ball. In 1910 he batted .385, with sixty-five stolen bases. In 1911 he had the best hitting year of his life. He made 248 hits, a batting average of .420, with 144 runs batted in and eighty-three stolen bases. The most bizarre aspect of his record was the psychology he used to win the batting title.

Late that season he and Shoeless Joe Jackson, who was considered a "friend" of Cobb's, were locked in a duel for the title. Detroit came into Cleveland for a six-game series. Cobb had worked out a strategy to handle Jackson. On the first day of the series the two teams were on the field before the start of the game and Jackson walked up to Cobb with a smile on his face.

"How are you, Ty?" he said.

Cobb's face turned red. "Stay away from me!" he growled.

"What the matter?" Jackson asked, surprised.

"Just keep out of my way," Cobb said.

It went that way through the whole series, Cobb snarling at Jackson, and Joe at a loss to explain Ty's actions. He became so confused he went hitless the first three games of the series—while Cobb was hitting everything.

The season ended with Cobb at .420, Jackson at .408. "I stole that title from Jackson," Cobb boasted later. "If I had waited for nature to take its course, he would have beaten me. I had to come up with something."

Cobb was always coming up with something. He always thought of the game in scientific terms. If he went into a batting slump, he reasoned that his stroke was off, so he just tried to hit the ball back to the pitcher, meet it right in the middle in order to flatten out his stroke. After a day or so of meeting the ball that way, he would be out of his slump and begin hitting it where the pitchers couldn't reach it.

Everyone hated him, but everyone respected him, too. "I never saw anyone like Cobb," said Casey Stengel, who played in the same era. "When he wiggled those wild eyes at a pitcher, you knew you were looking at the one bird nobody could beat. It was like he was superhuman."

Everyone felt that way. Early in the 1912 season, Cobb did something that made a Philadelphia sportswriter a believer. This is the way he wrote about it:

"Tyrus Cobb beat out a single down the first-base line, stole second, then shouted in warning that he would steal third and proceeded to do so. Then, with two strikes on the batter, Cobb broke for the plate. The pitch was a little high and before the catcher could pull it down, Cobb slid home. The man at the plate hadn't swung at the ball, but Cobb had gone all away around the bases!"

That was another year for Cobb, his second straight .400 year (a .410 average this time). He also had another king-size rhubarb.

The Tigers were playing in Highland Park New York against the "Highlanders," who were later to be known as the Yankees. The stands were packed and in one section along the left-field foul line was a choral group of anti-Cobbers. Inning after inning, they serenaded Ty. One man in particular was riding Cobb very hard. Cobb tried his best to ignore him but, finally, he burst.

He trotted down the left-field line, turned as if to go into center, heard this character bellowing insults at him, stopped, swung around, and charged. Before they could separate Cobb, the fans were ready to storm onto the field, to go after Cobb. Detroit players stood along the line with bats in their hands.

Cobb was tossed out of the game, and indefinitely suspended. That caused an amazing chain reaction. The entire Detroit team met a few days later and decided to go out on strike unless Cobb was reinstated. They did this out of no love for Cobb, but out of respect for his talents and what he could do for the team.

On May 18, manager Hughie Jennings was unable to field a team against the Athletics. Frank Navin, the Detroit owner, told Jennings to go out and get some sort of a team together. Some team, it was. Jennings hired Philadelphia semi-pros, sandlot players, college boys. The Athletics beat Detroit, 24-2.

Ban Johnson cancelled the next Detroit game and called the players together. "Unless this team reports for its scheduled game in Washington on May 21," he said, "I will drive every single one of you out of baseball."

It was Ty Cobb, himself, who finally emerged as peacemaker. He told the team to do as Johnson had ordered. They did. Cobb was fined $50 and suspended for ten days. Later that year, as an offshoot to the incident, he and his wife were attacked by three men as the Cobbs were driving to the railroad station. The men jumped on the running board of the car and one of them slashed at Ty with a knife, cutting him badly. Cobb stopped the car and not only fought off his attackers, he went after them. He made his train and the next day he played in a bloodsoaked, makeshift bandage. He hit a double and a triple, and only then was treated for the knife wound.

This was the only way he knew how to live: Fight if attacked, fight, anyway. Fight, fight, fight. "I did it for my father who was an exalted man," Cobb said much later. "He never got to see me play. But I knew he was watching, and I never let him down."

The years went by and Cobb fought on and could

not be defeated. In 1913 he batted .390. In 1914 he batted .368. In 1915, he batted .369, and stole his ninety-six bases, which was a record that held up for forty-seven years, until Maury Wills came along.

As he got older, he certainly did not get mellower. But he did seem to get smarter. He took care of himself. In spring training he wore weighted shoes because it would make him work harder, make him speedier when he switched to light shoes. He was the first hitter to swing three bats when warming up before approaching the plate, to make his bat feel lighter. He practiced sliding all the time, not only to keep sharp but also to toughen up his hide. At bat, he kept that sliding stance, his hands six inches apart on the bat, his feet planted close together so that he could lean into a pitch and hit it anywhere.

He took a completely scientific approach to everything about the game, and nobody knew how to stop him. Once Connie Mack, the manger of the Athletics, asked his catcher, Wally Schang, "Now suppose Cobb was on second and you knew he was going to steal third. What would you do?"

"Why, that's easy, Mr. Mack," Schang answered brightly, "I'd call for a pitchout, fake a throw to third, hold on to the ball, and try to tag the bum as he slid home."

Cobb finally lost a batting title in 1916, though he hit .371 (Tris Speaker hit .386). Then he came back the next three years and won three more, with averages of .383, .382, .384 (how was that for consistency?). He also had time in this period of World War I to join the Army briefly and work his way up to captain in the Chemical Warfare Division.

By 1921 he was considered, at thirty-five, an old ballplayer. He was suffering from a fractured rib, torn ligaments, battle scars all over his body, and aches that took longer and longer to go away. But he would not quit. That year he took over as playing manager of the Tigers.

The year before, the Tigers had finished seventh. They moved up only to sixth in 1921, even though Cobb batted .389, and a teammate, Harry Heilmann, batted .394. In 1923 he moved the club to second place.

Now, though, he was definitely getting tired. He had been unable to bring the Tigers another pennant. He was getting old. Worse, the game was changing. A young man by the name of Babe Ruth was changing the game from one of small skills—of the carefully placed hit, the bunt, the steal, the hit-and-run—to power, to the home run. "I guess," Cobb said sarcastically, "more fans would rather watch Ruth clout one over the fence than watch me steal a base."

After the 1926 season he announced his retirement as a player. He was forty years old. But Connie Mack offered him a $60,000 salary to play with the Athletics and Cobb, who liked money, couldn't resist.

He played two years more. He played like a man half his age. In 1927 he batted .357 and stole twenty-two bases. The next year he hit .323 and, then, it was over. Forty-two years old, he quit for good.

He quit with records as follows: He had played in 3,033 games. He had made 4,191 hits, scored 2,244 runs. He had stolen a total of 892 bases. He had sure credentials for baseball immortality.

The baseball Hall of Fame was completed at

Cooperstown in 1939 and the first memento to be hung in the museum was a pair of shoes with gleaming spikes. They belonged to Ty Cobb, of course.

His last years, unfortuntely, were sad years. He married twice, and both marriages ended in divorce. He lost two of his three sons in the prime of their lives. As he grew old, disease enveloped him. He had a leaky heart, infected bowels, diabetes, nervous tension; finally, cancer.

He had lost most of his friends, too, because as the years went on his disposition became even worse. He became even more caustic. He found he simply could not live with people. His biographer, Al Stump, called Cobb "the greatest, and the strangest, of all American sports figures."

From his $4 million fortune, he built and endowed hospitals and created the Cobb Educational Foundation to finance needy children through college. Yet when he'd get a fan letter, he would burn it in his fireplace. "Saves on firewood," he'd grumble.

In his last days, working with Stump on his autobiography, he told the writer what he wanted his book to stand for. "Give 'em the word," said Ty Cobb. "I had to fight all my life to survive. They were all against me . . . tried every dirty trick to cut me down. But I beat the————and left them in the ditch. Make sure the book says that."

Then the dying seventy-five-year-old man's features softened slightly. "What about it?" he asked Stump, "do you think they'll remember me?"

Stump said, "They'll always remember you."

On July 8, 1961, Al Stump received a letter from Cobb. It contained a photograph of Ty's mausoleum on the hillside in the Royston cemetery. On the front of the photo, Cobb had scrawled these words: "Any time now."

Nine days later, he was dead.

Bob Cousy

Boston, 1950: Red Auerbach speaking before his first press conference after being hired as coach of the Boston Celtics: "My first draft choice is going to be Charlie Share of Bowling Green." "Charlie Share?" screeches a Boston sportswriter, unbelieving. "What about Bob Cousy?" Auerbach turns to Walter Brown, owner of the Celtics, and says, "Am I supposed to win or am I supposed to worry about the local yokels?"

*　　　*　　　*

Los Angeles, 1963: Red Auerbach, pointing to Bob Cousy, who has just played the last game of his career: "You know, I've seen a lot of things. The man there—that man is the greatest athlete of them all."

YOU COULDN'T blame Arnold "Red" Auerbach for not wanting to take Cousy back in 1950. Bob, an All-American graduate of Holy Cross, stood only 6 feet 1 inches tall. He was giving away half a foot in height to most of the other players in the National Basketball Association. A "little" man didn't stand a chance in pro basketball. Besides, the Celtics were desperate for a big man. Charlie Share was a seven-footer, big and strong. "If it had been me," Bob Cousy wrote in his book, *The Last, Loud Roar,* I would have made exactly the same decision. When you need a big man and you have a chance to get him, there's no other choice you can make."

But there was another reason why Auerbach was reluctant to take Cousy. In college, Bob had been a flashy ballplayer. He had invented the spectacular behind-the-back pass. He was a dribbler, a driver. He passed and fed and faked like a magician. And he shot like a magician—twisting layups, sweeping hooks, off-balance one-handers. How would this kind of play fit into the "big league?"

Well, it didn't take thirteen years for Red Auerbach to become a believer about Bob Cousy. It didn't take that long at all. When Cousy, through a circumstance no less freakish than a draw of the hat, did finally become a member of the Boston Celtics, Red Auerbach found out right away that first season of 1950-51 what he had.

The whole league found out, and at first they didn't know if they could take it. Pro basketball was stunned, bewildered. There were anguished cries of "bush." A rookie, Bob Cousy, was revolutionizing the game. He was doing more. He was *making* the pro game. But it was hard to see at first.

On January 14, 1951, the Celtics met the Philadelphia Warriors in the Boston Arena. At stake was first place in the Eastern Division. With two minutes left, the Celtics clung to a slight lead. Red Auerbach called a time out and huddled with his team.

"I want you to give it to Cousy," he said, "give it to Cousy."

Sonny Hertzberg passed the ball out to Bob Donham. Donham dribbled upcourt, then passed to Cousy. Bob went into his dance. He began bouncing the ball, moving slowly, waiting for the Warriors to come to him. Nelson Bobb ran up and lunged at the ball. Cousy switched hands and dribbled around him, moving toward the basket. Suddenly, he shifted and dribbled back toward midcourt.

The Warriors' George Senesky swiped at the ball and Cousy slapped it and kept possession.

Now it was Nelson Bobb's turn again. He dived at Cousy. He fouled Cousy. Bob went to the line and sunk the shot.

The Warriors started downcourt and lost the ball. Again, it was passed to Cousy. Again, Cousy went into his act. He dribbled up to the foul line, and into the corner. Senesky moved in on him from one side, Bobb from the other. "Cooz" fell to a knee, dribbling all the while. Bouncing up, he banged the ball between Bobb and Senesky, came out of the crush and picked up the dribble again.

Lazy Joe Fulks, 6 foot 5 inches, roared in on Cousy. He circled his massive arms around Bob's body, though not enough to foul Cousy. Bob was unable to move forward or sideways. So he tapped the ball behind his back with his right hand and picked it up with his left without losing a bounce. In an instant he was away from Fulks.

He kept on dribbling and the Warriors became desperate—no, hysterical! They began to foul Cousy. In less than two minutes Bob was fouled five times. Each time he made his foul shot, each shot put the Celtics that far ahead. The game ended 97-87, and Bob Cousy had scored thirty-four points.

Afterward, the Warrior players sat in their dressing room, stunned. "I've never seen anything like it," Senesky said. "Not in this league, anyway."

"It's no good," said Philadelphia owner Eddie Gott-lieb. "It's no good for the league."

But it was good for the league—it helped the league grow, because people wanted to come and see the little David show up the Goliaths of pro basketball; people wanted to pay their money to see Bob Cousy.

And if it was good for the league, it was certainly good for the Boston Celtics. Give credit to the coach, Red Auerbach. Give credit to the big man, Bill Russell. Give credit to the gifted players like Tommy Heinsohn, Bill Sharman, Frank Ramsey, Sam Jones. But it was Bob Cousy who lit the fuse on what turned out to be the greatest dynasty pro basketball had ever known. It was Bob Cousy, playmaker, court general, driving force, who led the Celtics to seven straight Eastern Division championships and five straight NBA titles. In thirteen seasons of professional basketball, Bob Cousy established himself as one of the greatest players the game has ever known.

The whole record is one of superlatives. Cousy was the only player named to the all-NBA team for ten successive seasons (and he was twice named to the second team). In his thirteen seasons he participated in thirteen All-Star games, and was voted the Most Valuable Player in two of them.

Through the 1965-66 season, Bob remained fourth among pro basketball's all-time scorers. And of the three men above him—Wilt Chamberlain, Dolph Schayes, Bob Pettit—the smallest, Schayes, was seven inches taller than Cousy.

In his lifetime, Bob scored 16,955 points on 6,167 field goals (third in the NBA all-time ranks) and 4,621 foul shots (fourth among the all-timers). He is in second place in most games played, 917, and first in most minutes played, 30,230 (a record that will probably be broken by Bob's old teammate, Bill Russell).

That was Bob Cousy the scorer, one of the all-time leaders in pro basketball. But couple that with Cousy the playmaker—his 6,949 assists is far and away the most in the NBA—and you have the most devastating combination ever seen in the game.

Scoring, actually, was a secondary preoccupation for Cousy. "I never looked for a shooting percentage," he once said. "I took my shots as they came; hooks, drives, long pushes—whatever presented itself at the time. I could have tried for the good position shot and hit well over .400, I believe, but that never entered my mind. The team always came first.

"It's winning alone that counts," Cousy continued. "Whether I had 715 assists, as I did one year, or 7,000, if we didn't win the title or get into the finals, it meant nothing to me."

Bob Cousy applies that philosophy today as a college coach. The object of the game, he tells his students, is to win. Bob Cousy should be a very good coach, if he is listened to, and if he can pass on the strength of his own desire to his players. For it was that desire, that burning will to excel, that carried Bob Cousy such a long, long way.

"I was born and brought up in Yorkville in the East

80's, in New York," Bob writes in *The Last, Loud Roar,* "and in those days I played no basketball at all. My day was spent playing stickball, stealing from fruitstands, and swimming in the East River."

It was the typical early childhood of a boy born in a big city in a Depression. His date of birth, August 9, 1928, was just a year before the stock market crash that signaled the end of one era, an era of good times, to another era, an era of hard times.

Bob's parents had only recently arrived from France, and Joseph Cousy got a job driving a taxi while Juliette Cousy took charge of the house and looked after her only child. Bob was called "Flenchy" by his friends then, which was really "Frenchy," except that Bob had trouble pronouncing his r's. He went to a parochial school in the neighborhood and he was a good student. He was also a good athlete in those days. He played everything, it seemed, but basketball.

The basketball began when he was twelve, when the Cousys moved to a house in St. Albans, Long Island. The Cousys were able to own the house only by living in the cellar, sleeping in the attic, and renting out both the first and second floors.

In 1942, Bob entered Andrew Jackson High School and tried out for the junior varsity team. He was one of 250 kids who tried out, and he didn't make it. He was only 5 feet 8 inches, skinny, green, and shy. Besides, the coach was looking for tall boys.

He tried out again, and failed again. The third time he did make the team but only, he remembers, because he had fallen out of a tree and broken his right wrist. "I had to play baseball and handball and anything else that came along with my left hand," he said. "By the time I began to play basketball shortly afterward, my left hand was so strong that I'd be shooting almost as much left-handed as right."

Halfway through his sophomore year, the Andrew Jackson coach, Lou Grummond, saw Cousy playing in a community center. He thought that Bob was a natural left-hander and he came over and asked Cousy to fill the No. 1 position on the junior varsity. Bob had to confess that he was a right-hander, but Grummond told him to come, anyway.

As a junior, Bob played only a few games for the varsity. He had flunked a course in citizenship (for talking in class) and was ineligible until the next marking term, which was in February. On his next report card he got an A in citizenship and joined the team.

He was an immediate sensation, scoring twenty-eight points in his first game, and going on from there. And he was even better as a senior. He led Jackson to the Queens Division championship. Going into his last game, he needed a twenty-one point performance to win the New York City high school scoring championship. His average that season had been seventeen points, but he was determined. In the team's last game against Far Rockaway, Bob scored twenty-eight points. After only a season and a half of high school basketball, Cousy was the New York City scoring champion. Later, he was selected captain of the city all-scholastic team.

Despite such blue-chip statistics, Bob was virtually ignored by the college recruiters. It was 1946 and the boys were coming back from World War II into college, so that there wasn't as great a demand for boys out of high school. Also, there wasn't that tremendous recruiting push that would start soon and grow out of all proportions as the years went by. In addition, Bob wasn't a big boy. At the time he was just 6 feet tall, shy and skinny, his eyes eager, his shoulders narrow, his curly black hair thick, and his face so smooth he didn't have to shave every day.

He was eager all right. He needed a scholarship because his parents could not afford to send him to college. At last he was visited by General Al McClellan, the coach of Boston College. McClellan came in and talked to Bob and talked to his parents and offered Bob a full scholarship—room, board and books. Bob went to Boston and visited the campus and he was disappointed because B.C. had no dormitories. The thought of having to live with a strange family, he admitted, petrified him. But, still, if no other offer came along, Boston College it would be.

Then he got a call from an ex-Jackson player, Ken Haggerty, who was now playing with Holy Cross. Holy Cross was coming into New York to play and Haggerty set up a meeting between Cousy and the Holy Cross coach, Doggie Julian. The two men and Julian offered Bob the same deal as B.C. a straight scholarship. When Julian told Cousy that Holy Cross had dormitories, Bob's mind was made up. He went home and talked to his parents and they gave their consent.

In the fall of 1946, freshmen were eligible to play for the varsity and Bob just made the second team. Holy Cross had built a powerhouse and went on to win the national title. Bob didn't play as much as he hoped but he did score 227 points. "There's so much to learn about this game," Bob told sportswriter Al Hirshberg that spring. "I wish I could learn it all at once. I wonder if I'll live long enough to know all there is to know about it."

He was learning. In the '47-48 season Bob was a regular, and he and Kaftan spearheaded another strong team. Bob doubled his point total, to 486, and people were beginning to notice him.

In his junior year, in one game, Bob Cousy became known all over the country.

A strong Loyola of Chicago team came into Boston to play Holy Cross at the Boston Garden. The year before, Holy Cross had beaten Loyola when Cousy scored twelve points in the last four and a half minutes. Now Loyola was prepared to handle Cousy.

With a minute to go the score was tied, 57-57. Buster Sheary, the new Holy Cross coach, had given the team its instructions: Have Cousy drive in and if he didn't get the basket he'd still have a good chance of picking up a foul, and probably a two-shooter.

But Loyola had expected just that and Cousy was covered as tight as a cork in a bottle. With twenty seconds to go, Bob started driving into the key from the left side of the court. Most of the time that night Bob had been going to his right, so his opponent was now playing him that way. If "Cooz" had straightened out at the key and driven right in, as he was supposed to, he would have run right over the Loyola man. If he tried to swing around him, taking the long route around, he would have ended up out near the baseline, a very difficult shot.

Without thinking at all, he slapped the ball behind his back with his right hand, picked up the dribble with his left hand and, as he changed direction, put up a left-handed shot. He was still closely covered and he got off the shot awkwardly—but it went in.

In the locker room moments later, Cousy sat dazed. He had just invented a new maneuver—the behind-the-back pass—but he couldn't explain it. "It just came the moment the situation forced me into it," he told reporters. "It was purely and simply one of those cases when necessity is the mother of invention. I was absolutely amazed myself at what I had done."

The spectators were just as amazed and now had something more to come out for. They were coming out now not only to see Holy Cross in action, but to see Bob Cousy in action, to see his sleight-of-hand magic—his behind-the-back dribble or his over-the-shoulder pass, which he had also developed.

That season Holy Cross won nineteen games and lost eight and Bob Cousy was an All-American. He scored 480 points, and his three-year total of 1,193 was a Holy Cross record.

He was even better as a senior. In one early-season game against Trinity he scored twenty points in less than twenty minutes. The Trinity coach, Ray Oesting, could only shake his head in awe. "I've seen all the college stars of this game," Ray said, "but Cousy is far ahead of anyone. He is so far out of this basketball world that it's hard to compare him with anyone."

With Cousy leading the way, Holy Cross ran off twenty-six straight wins, ended with a 27-2 record. Bob had scored 582 points and unanimously become All-American. And now he was hopeful of taking his show on to the pros.

But when he was snubbed by Red Auerbach and the

Boston Celtics, he wasn't at all sure about his future. Bob was picked by Tri-Cities in the 1950 draft and went to the Chicago Stags in a trade. Then the Stags folded. The Stag roster had to be distributed throughout the rest of the NBA. The dispersal of the players went along smoothly until it came to the three back-courtmen on the Stags—Max Zaslofsky, Andy Phillip and the rookie, Bob Cousy.

Of the three, Zaslofsky was considered the best pro, with Phillip next. Cousy was strictly an unknown quantity. Three NBA owners, Ned Irish of the New York Knicks, Eddie Gottlieb of the Philadelphia Warriors, and Walter Brown of the Celtics argued throughout the night. All wanted Zaslofsky. Finally, NBA president Maurice Podoloff put a stop to it.

"I'm sick and tired of all this," he said. "There are three of you and three players; all backcourtmen. I'm going to put their names in a hat, and whoever you draw, that's who you get."

Ned Irish drew first: Zaslofsky. Walter Brown drew next: Cousy. He left the meeting tired and angry. "I figured," he said later, "that I'd gotten the dirty end of the stick all around."

So Bob Cousy was a Boston Celtic after all and it was the luckiest, luck of the Irish. From the beginning, Cooz was a sensation. One Boston columnist wrote about Cousy that year: "His behind-the-back passes and his unorthodox whirling dervish shots haven't proved detrimental. He has brought the Celtics not only color but he has also given them the spark, drive and extra punch to set the Eastern Division pace."

The Celtics finished second in the East, but the season before they had finished last. Things were looking up. In his second season as a pro, Bob really established himself. His 1,433 points was good for third in the league and his 441 assists good for second.

In the 1952-53 season, Bob finished first in assists, with 547, and third in scoring with 1,407 points. And then, in a memorable playoff game, he reached new heights.

In the Eastern Division opening series, the Celtics beat Syracuse in the first game. But they trailed in the second game by one point with seconds left. Cousy, who already had twenty-four points, came out of a mid-court crush, bouncing the ball in front of him. With a quick flick, he sent the ball soaring to a teammate who stood free beneath the basket. The ball flew out of bounds and Cousy was marked as the goat. All Syracuse had to do was hold the ball and the game would be over.

Suddenly, the Celtics stole the ball. A pass to Cousy. Bob dribbled fast, looking for an opponent. He was hacked by a Syracuse player. Foul. One shot.

He stood at the line calmly. He bounced the ball, aimed it, and released it. The ball soared up, dropped down and floated into the basket. The game was tied at 77, and an overtime was coming up.

With seconds remaining in the overtime, Cousy had scored five of his team's eight points, but it hadn't been enough. Syracuse had scored nine. But Bob was fouled again. Once more he went to the line and once more he made his shot. And once more, an overtime. Syracuse scored, then the Celtics, then Syracuse again. The pressure was intense but Cousy remained calm. He drove in, stopped, shot, and scored. It was 90-90. A third overtime.

Syracuse applied the pressure again. They roared to the front. With thirteen seconds left, it seemed all over; Syracuse led by five points. But Cousy, tireless, alert, at his physical and emotional peak, would not give up. Scientists once made a test on Cousy. The tests showed that Bob's adrenal glands manufactured huge quantities of a pair of particular hormones. Scientists said these hormones were associated with vigilance, alertness, self-control, aggressivenes, anger and combativeness. In this vital game against Syracuse, with the pressure stacked to exploding point, Bob Cousy was pumping out those hormones.

He dribbled downcourt, bobbing, weaving, reaching midcourt and flinging up a one-hander. It went in—and he was fouled in the act of shooting. He sunk the foul and now the Celtics were down by just two.

Boston got the ball once more. Cousy took it with five seconds left. He dribbled across the midcourt line and his right hand swept up in a wild hook, arcing the ball towards the basket. The buzzer sounded, but the ball was in the air—and in the basket. Cousy had scored eight more of his team's nine points in the third overtime, and now a fourth overtime was necessary.

With two and a half minutes left, Syracuse took a five point lead and then they cracked. Bob Cousy had been too much for them. The Celtics scored twelve straight points—nine by Bob—and an 111-105 victory.

It was the biggest scoring night of Cousy's career. Fifty points. Twenty-five of them in the four overtimes.

In the Celtics' dressing room afterwards, Bob sat with his head buried in his hands. "I can't believe it's over," he said. "I can't believe it's over. I can't believe it's over."

In the 1953-54 season, Bob was the star of the NBA All-Star game, leading the East to a 98-93 victory over the West. He scored ten of his team's fourteen points in overtime, twenty points in all, and was named the game's Most Valuable Player. That season Bob again led the league in assists and was second in scoring.

Yet, the Celtics were going nowhere. The best they had been able to do was reach the Eastern Division finals, no farther. Red Auerbach hadn't yet been able to put it all together.

In 1956-57, he did.

The catalyst undoubtedly was Bill Russell, who joined the team in midseason after leading the United States to an Olympic basketball victory in Australia. Russell was the big man the team had needed for so long. He was the man with the strength and the stamina to be an overpowering rebounder. In addition, there were two other sparkling rookies, Tommy Heinsohn and Frank Ramsey.

There was also Bob Cousy who was now at his best.

He was twenty-eight years old and could do everything and the only question was, how did he do so much? How was it possible for a man of his size to stay in there, to excel night after night against men so much bigger than he? Bob Cousy said it was because he was a "freak."

He was referring to his body, which may have been unusual but was hardly freakish. Bob's hands were large, his fingers long; he held a basketball easily in one hand. His arms were long, too, which helped him dribble so close to the floor. Slim from the waist up (he weighed 180 to 185 pounds), Cousy had strong, heavy legs, legs that were meant for endurance tests like the constant sprints up and down a basketball court. He also had peripheral vision, which enabled him to see in a straight-ahead glance on either side of him. He had one other thing, too—a cold, absolute assurance in his own ability.

He carried that assurance to its heights in the 1956-57 season. It was a season when he scored 1,319 points, when his 478 assists were the league's best for the fifth straight season. It was a season in which he was not only named most valuable player in the All-Star game, but also, at the end of the year, the NBA championship.

They met the St. Louis Hawks in the finals. This was the Hawks of Bob Pettit, Cliff Hagan, Slater Martin. This was a basketball team, too.

In the first game Cousy scored twenty-six points but the Hawks won in two overtimes, 125-123. Boston won the next night 110-98 and Cousy scored twenty-two. The Hawks won the third game in St. Louis, 100-98, on a last-second hook shot by Bob Pettit. Boston came back to win the fourth game 123-118 as Cousy poured in thirty-one points.

Back in Boston the Celtics won a game and St. Louis won the next one and now there was nowhere to go. Each team had won three games. Each team had played to its limit. Pettit was averaging better than thirty points a game for St. Louis. Heinsohn, Sharman and Cousy were all averaging better than twenty points per game. But now only one game counted.

It was a beauty. It went two overtimes, it literally

went down to the last second, the Celtics finally winning it, 125-123, and their first NBA championship.

Bob Cousy today still remembers that as the greatest moment of his life, "the time when I hugged Auerbach and he hugged me back when the gun went off, and we won our first championship. That was the one we wanted so badly."

The glory years were still ahead of Bob Cousy and the Celtics. They lost the title to St. Louis in 1957-58, and then they came back and started a streak that was to continue even past Cousy's retirement. But Cousy wasn't yet thinking of retiring. Every season he was magnificent. Every season he seemed to do something that set him apart from the others in the league.

For instance, in 1959 Wilt Chamberlain came into the league. The first Celtic-Philadelphia contest was billed as a Chamberlain-Russell battle. But it was Cousy who stole the show with twenty-four points and thirteen assists.

That same year he scored a record twenty-eight assists in a Boston victory over Minneapolis, and his season's assists, 715, was a new record.

In 1960, now thirty-two years old, Bob played against Oscar Robertson for the first time, a new challenge. Oscar, the Big O, had come into the league billed as the "new" Cousy. He was taller than Bob, he was 6 feet 5 inches, but he was a backcourtman, a playmaker and a scorer.

They played against each other for the first time in Boston in November. Before the game, Bob sat by his locker and talked about the challenge. "It's pride," Bob said. "I've thought a lot about it all week long and talked to myself about it. Better get yourself up, Bob.

Better be at your best, Bob. Oscar's coming to town to play in *your* arena, before *your* crowd, for the first time."

It was a near standoff. Robertson scored thirty-one points. Cousy scored thirty. Each man had seven assists, and Bob outrebounded Robertson seven to six. The Celtics won the game, 136-120.

But he was thirty-two years old now and he was tired. He was married, he had two lovely daughters, and he was getting weary of the long NBA schedule, the tiring road trips. He wanted to see more of his family, watch his girls grow up, and settle down to a more normal life. He announced, finally, that the 1962-63 season would be his last.

And it was, and he went out a winner with another championship team.

Everywhere over the league, they had a "day" for Bob Cousy, a farewell to this great gladiator who had done so much for professional basketball. The most emotional scene of course was at home in Boston Garden, where he was showered with gifts and with love from the Boston fans. In his speech he spoke of his love for everyone who had been so good to him, and of his regret that it was all coming to an end. Someone in the balcony yelled down, "We love you, Cooz," and Bob Cousy heard it and wept. Then his speech was over and the fans stood up and cheered and clapped and whistled for over three minutes.

His final game was the Celtics' final game of the year in Los Angeles against the Lakers. It was the sixth playoff game. A Celtic victory would mean a fifth straight NBA championship.

Boston led 92-88 when Cousy fell heavily to the floor trying to run backward to keep up with the

Lakers' Dick Barnett. Terrible pain shot up to his left ankle. It hurt so badly that he had to roll over on his right side to take all the weight off it. He looked up at the clock and said to himself, "Ten minutes too soon. Ten minutes too soon."

He was helped to the bench, to the very end of the bench. He sat there in pain and watched as Los Angeles began a comeback. He watched the screaming partisan crowd of 15,000 on their feet, cheering and shouting for the Lakers. He watched as the Celtics lead shrunk to one point. Then he could watch no longer.

He got up and walked towards Red Auerbach. Auerbach looked surprised.

"How's it feel?" he asked.

"I think I can go," Cousy said.

The ankle still pained him, but he was thinking: this is the time they need somebody to assume the responsibilities of a playmaker. They're used to having me in there, bringing up the ball and calling the plays. It's important psychologically that they feel everything's in its place and everyone's doing their job.

So he went in, and the Celtics steadied and with three seconds left they held a 112-109 lead and, now, Bob Cousy knew it was all over.

Sam Jones threw him the ball from out of bounds. Bob took four long leaping strides upcourt and then, as the buzzer sounded, rip-sawing through the tumult of noise, he threw the ball into the air. He threw the ball high up the rafters thanking God—as he said later —that he had been allowed to leave a champion.

Bob Cousy had left the game, had left pro baskebtall forever, as a champion.

Jesse Owens

THE YOUNG BOY and the older man were walking slowly in the ninety-five degree heat to their entrance at the Stadio Olimpico in Rome. Suddenly, the boy stopped and gripped the arm of the man.

Guarda!" he said in Italian. *"Veda questa uomo?"* —see that man?

"Si," said the man, looking at a knot of people who were surrounding a Negro. *"Ch'e? Who is it?"*

"Jesse Owens!" the boy said excitedly. "Jesse Owens!"

"Ah, Jesse Owens." The man, this middle-aged man who had lived in Italy all his life, stopped and looked and his face became the face of a man who has just entered church. He steered the boy towards the cluster of American tourists who were taking autographs from Jesse Owens. He pulled out a blank piece of paper and a pen.

The boy moved in close to Owens and said, "Would you mind signing an autograph for my uncle? He's Italian. But he remembers you, he remembers you very well."

Jesse Owens, forty-six years old this day in 1960, smiled. His face was lined with the telltale marks of his age, but it was somehow a young face still, the face of

an athlete. He signed his name and *he* said, "thank
you," and the boy's uncle said, *"grazie,"* and off they
went into the great Olympic Stadium. And that afternoon, under a blazing Italian sun, they watched Ralph
Boston broad jump 26 feet 7 and ¾ inches and break
the last of Jesse Owens' Olympic records. They
watched with pleasure for Boston, but it was pleasure
mingled with regret. The regret was for the man who
had just given them a remembrance. And perhaps the
man thought back to twenty-four years, when the
scene was Berlin, Germany, when the world was just a
little different.

It was Jesse Owens' second appearance in the
Olympics of 1936. A day earlier he had taken his first
gold medal, winning the 100 meters in the world-
record tying time of 10.3s. That victory had met with
the disapproval of Adolf Hitler, the Chancellor of
Germany. Adolf Hitler had definite ideas about what a
champion should be made of. Hitler's definition of a
champion was an "Aryan"—a superman of pure white
stock. Hitler's Aryans were "the master race." From a
Nazi point of view a champion certainly was not the
seventh son of an impoverished Alabama cotton
picker. A champion was certainly not a non-Aryan
American Negro. Jesse Owens had slashed at Hitler's
pet theory and now he was back again, trying to slash
farther in the broad jump, his real specialty.

That morning in the qualifying finals, he almost
didn't make it.

The qualifying mark was only 23 feet, 5½ inches,
and Jesse could do that normally in his sleep. But he
was overconfident. On his first try he stormed down

the runway—and kept running, right through the pit. The officials ruled a foul.

On his second try, he fouled again, taking off beyond the board. Now he was worried. One more foul and he would be out of the competition; he would be finished. He kicked disgustedly at the dirt. Did I come three thousand miles for this? he asked himself, to foul out of the trials and make a fool of myself?

Suddenly, he felt a hand on his shoulder. He turned to look into the friendly blue eyes of a tall German broad jumper. "I'm Luz Long," the German said, shaking hands with Owens.

Luz Long was Hitler's best in this event and he had come over to give Jesse Owens some advice.

"You should be able to qualify with your eyes closed," Long said. "Why don't you draw a line a few inches in back of the board and aim at making your takeoff from there? You'll be sure not to foul, and you certainly ought to jump far enough to qualify."

The truth of what he said hit Jesse. He drew a line a full foot in back of the board. He jumped and qualified with almost a foot to spare.

That afternoon, with Hitler and his criminal cronies Goebbels and Goering sharing his box, with 100,000 spectators screaming in excitement, the broad jump came down to a duel between Jesse Owens, the non-Aryan, and Luz Long, the Aryan. It was a stirring duel. Owens set an Olympic record on his second jump and Long tied it on his fifth—of six—jumps. But Owens had more left. On both his fifth and sixth tries, Jesse Owens lengthened his Olympic record. His final jump was measured at 26 feet, 5¼ inches. At that moment, Luz Long came alongside of Owens, beaten. He smiled and congratulated Jesse Owens and put his arm around the American Negro. At that moment Hitler and his gang rose abruptly and left the Stadium. They had had enough.

Jesse Owens never forgot that act of friendship. Luz Long was killed in Sicily in World War II fighting for his country and, after the war, Owens revisited Germany and made it a point to visit Long's widow and son and to tell Long's boy what kind of a man his father was.

So the feelings of the American boy and the Italian man in the Olympic Stadium in Rome, 1960, were a mixture of gladness for Ralph Boston and sadness for Jesse Owens. Jesse Owens' own emotions, watching his last great record die, were different. The memories were of Berlin, of 1936, of Luz Long, of triumph and glory. And now there was the sense of loss, and loss not just of his own record. After Boston's record had been certified, Jesse Owens attempted to explain his feelings:

"I learned very early," he said, "not to hang my hat on a few gold medals and fieldhouse plaques. But by the same token I got kind of used to having that old record around. It was something having people come up to me on the streets every four years and ask, 'Do you think they'll do it this time, Jesse? Will they ever do it?' I was grateful for that.

"More than any other records I set or gold medals I won, that broad jump mark began to add up bigger and bigger for me through the years. It became a real part of me—a living thing in itself and like any living thing it had to die. It finally did die but the funeral wasn't a sad one. It was the same as when a ninety-three year-old man finally passes away. You can't cry over it. You're glad that he lived as long as he did."

Jesse Owens' records are all dead now, all but one. After thirty-two years his national scholastic record in the 100 meters (9.4s) has not yet been broken. That one will die, too, someday, but it doesn't really matter because the man, the man who set all those records, is immortal. His achievements will never die.

In 1964, sixty-two of the country's leading track and field coaches were polled by *Sport* Magazine to pick the all-time track and field team. Jesse Owens was named on top in the 100-yard dash, the 220, the broad jump. He was also picked as "the greatest performer in track and field history." There was little debate. Owens got eight times as many votes as his nearest competitor. One of the finest tributes came from his former coach, Larry Snyder of Ohio State:

"He ruled four events (also the low hurdles) though he had only two years of college competition. He was so superior to his contemporaries that had he continued as present-day athletes do his performances might never have been surpassed."

But what if he were running at his peak today, in the space age? "It wouldn't matter," said Colgate University coach John Warner. "He would still be on top. Under present conditions he would have improved his records."

Those records—eight Big Ten and eight NCAA championships; four Olympic gold medals; four Olympic records. All were compiled in a glorious two-year period.

The preparation, of course, took a lifetime.

He was born in 1915 in Alabama and his parents were poor and picked cotton. When he was six James Cleveland Owens helped his father and older brothers with the cotton picking. A few years later his father moved the family to Cleveland, Ohio, to take a job as a laborer in a steel mill. The boy reported to grammar school in Cleveland and his teacher asked, "What is your first name?"

"J. C., ma'am."

"Jessie?" she said.

"Yes, ma'am, Jessie," he replied, untroubled by the thought of having a new name. It became Jesse Owens from that time on.

At the age of thirteen he ran his first formal race, a forty-yard dash. He lost. "I got left in the holes," he told writer Myron Cope. He even remembered the name of the boy who had beaten him, Johnny Young. But he didn't lose much after that.

In high school he set the national scholastic record for the 100-yard dash, the 9.4s record that still stands. He might possibly have done better but he ran in those days on an empty stomach. It was the Depression and his family was desperately poor. Jesse's father had had his leg smashed in an auto accident and was unable to work for years, and with eight children to raise there was never enough to eat. Jesse remembers his childhood as an "existence," that's all.

But he worked hard in school and was able to enter Ohio State University without an athletic scholarship. He got a job running a night elevator in the State office building from 5 P.M. to 12:30 A.M. for which he was paid $150 a month. After work he went to his rooming house, ate, and slept about four hours, rising each morning at 6:30 for an 8:30 class. It was a strange way to train but Jesse never minded it. "I got better marks that way," he recalled. "I had a chance to study on the elevator. I had forty minutes out of every hour to study. The crews—the charwomen—changed floors every hour. That took about twenty minutes. I had a good superintendent, and he gave me permission to study the rest of the time."

Larry Snyder, the Ohio State track coach, knew he had a good one the first time he saw Jesse in a track suit. "He was in perfect shape," Snyder remembered, "not an ounce of fat on his body. He had this high tension nervous system." Before competing, Jesse worked up such extraordinary tension that his adrenal glands flooded his bloodstream with adrenalin, which stimulated the heart. As a result, Owens had great strength under pressure.

He began to run nationally and almost at once he became a national figure.

As a sophomore in 1933 he broke the indoor broad-jump record of the national indoor AAU champion. He began to beat everyone in sprints. How did he do it? "I would stick with the field," Jesse once said, "breathing naturally, until thirty yards from the finish. Then I took one big breath, held it, tensed all my abdominal muscles and set sail."

Owens' one weakness was that he got off to a slow start. John Kieran, writing in the New York *Times,* had a unique theory. "Ordinarily," Kieran wrote, "he let his rivals get a fair start on him . . . possibly to make it a fair race and give the spectators a thrill." This was nonsense. It was a quirk of Jesse's that instead of concentrating on the gun at the start, he would watch his rivals out of the corner of his eye. When they started, he started. But he caught up quickly. He had a relatively short but powerful seven-foot stride and when he went into high gear it was goodbye to all his rivals.

On May 25, 1935, he put it all together. He staged the most astounding one-man show in track history.

But he almost didn't get the chance to compete at all. A week before the Big Ten outdoor track and field championships, to be held in Ann Arbor, Michigan, Jesse was engaging in horseplay with some of his college mates when he slipped and fell down a flight of stairs. He felt the pain shoot up from his foot to his spine.

That week, Jesse practiced very little. The night before the Big Ten meet he was in a room in Ypsilanti, Michigan, with a chemical heating pad taped to his back and stomach so he would have heat all night. The next morning he climbed into a hot tub, then he dressed and sat down on a chair—and found he couldn't get up.

He was helped into the automobile that took him the ten miles to Ann Arbor. The pain was in his back, in his thighs, behind his knees. "I couldn't even warm up," he told writer Myron Cope. "There was a question of whether I could get down on my mark."

He decided to try the broad jump, anyway.

Standing far down the end of the lane, he flexed his knees, bent his body gingerly, winced, bent again, trotted down to the pit and stuck a piece of paper at the twenty-six foot mark. Then he trotted back to the starting position and did a short series of deep knee bends. The heck with it, he said to himself. I've got to try. He stripped off his sweat pants and was ready. His bronzed legs were as taut as a high wire. He weighed 165 pounds but there was not a bulge anywhere. His body was like a strip of corded steel. He was crippled but he didn't care. He started his run.

He churned down the lane, picking up speed as he went along. Thirteen yards from the take-off he sucked in deeply, held his breath and jumped. He soared into the air, his legs churning like a locomotive. And as he landed safely in the pit, he let out his breath.

Officials measured the jump at 26 feet, 8¼ inches. It was a world record.

But he was not finished. Now the pain was completely ignored as he ran the 100-yard dash in 9.4s, tying the world's record; as he ran the 200 in 20.3s, breaking the world's record; as he stepped the 220-yard low hurdles in 22.6s, breaking still another world's record. Although crippled and in terrible pain, Jesse Owens had nonetheless set three world's records and tied one all in one day.

"It was such a nice day," he told writer Cope. "And when I got down on my mark, all I thought about was the race. My back didn't hurt at all. Everything was fine."

Everything was fine indeed for Jesse Owens, and for the United States on the eve of the 1936 Olympics. Everything was fine because now the United States had a big ace in the hole, a superman of its own.

It was 1936 and in the United States, still suffering from the Depression, there was to be a Presidential election. The Republicans would nominate a Kansan, Alf Landon, to oppose Franklin Delano Roosevelt. In Europe in 1936 there were very few elections to be held. Benito Mussolini was the absolute Dictator of

Italy, Adolf Hitler was the absolute Dictator of Germany. And Hitler went about preparing the Olympics as a showcase for his own theories. A German, Max Schmeling, was heavyweight boxing champion of the world, and that was a start. Now Hitler, through the Olympic games, would really show the world what kind of supermen his Aryan athletes were.

Meanwhile, Larry Snyder was grooming Jesse Owens carefully for the Olympics. To prevent his star from burning himself out before the games, the coach deliberately curtailed Owens' activities during the preceding winter. Then, as the Olympics drew closer, Owens grew sharper. In the final American tryouts he won the 100-meter and 200-meter dashes and the broad jump. Just before leaving for Germany, Jesse Owens said, "Without being overconfident, I think I'll be a triple winner in the Olympics."

On August 3, 1936, the second day of the Olympic track and field program, Owens made a bid for his first gold medal. In a field of three Americans, one German, one Dutchman and one Swede, he was favored to win the 100-meter sprint.

When Owens stepped to the starting line in the 100-meter final, Hitler was in the stands. With him were Hermann Goering and Joseph Goebbels and Heinrich Himmler.

Jesse looked around him. He saw the green grass, the red track with the white lines. He looked up into the stands and saw 120,000 people sitting and standing within the great arena, and it was almost as though he could hear the stillness. He knew the 120,000 people were waiting breathlessly for the gun to roar, to send these perfectly conditioned athletes on their way in the most thrilling of all running races. His eyes wandered upward and he saw the flags of every nation that were represented in Berlin. And above the flags, the blue German sky, and he remembered his mother's last words—"Do right, Jesse, and do good."

The whistle blew and the starters received their final instructions. The starter stepped back about ten paces and he hollered in a loud gutteral voice, *"Auf-demplatz,"* and every man went to his mark.

Jesse Owens dug in and tensed, feeling "like your legs can't carry the weight of your body, your stomach's not there."

He was the first one down on the mark. And when the starter said in a soft voice, *"Fertig,"* the adrenalin began to work and the tension was unbearable.

The gun barked and Jesse Owens broke perfectly. The gun, he said later, was like a dry cell battery. "When you pour water on it you get power."

The power was there all right and Jesse broke into the lead. He heard them flanking him but they fell behind him. He was out there by himself and feeling the power and driving and wanting to run, run, run and never stop, feeling it in him to do what he had trained himself to do—run faster than any human being in the world.

At the halfway mark he led fellow American Frank Wykoff by a yard. Wykoff tried to come on but it was impossible and the effort cost him a medal and he drifted back to fourth place. Ralph Metcalfe of Marquette University made a tremendous bid in the last fifty meters but Jesse held him off, breaking the tape three feet ahead of Metcalfe. On a heavy track Jesse had tied the world's record of 10.3s. and it was, for him, "the greatest moment of my career."

But now the marvelous moments followed in quick succession. The following day he won his second gold medal in the broad jump. The day after the broad jump he ran in the 200-meter dash. He won easily—in 20.7 seconds, another Olympic record. Then, a few days later, he ran the first leg on the championship United States 400-meter relay team. He gave the American team an insurmountable lead and the quartet of Owens, Metcalfe, Draper and Wykoff set a new Olympic record.

Four gold medals for Jesse Owens, and now he was the toast of the whole world. After the Olympics there was a tour of the Continent, and there could have been more tours but Jesse wanted to come home. His weight had dropped from 163 to 147 pounds. He was tired and he had to make a decision about his future.

He had a year's eligibility left at Ohio State, but he had also been deluged by offers from sports promoters and theatrical bookers. Should he remain as an amateur or should he cash in on his fame? It was 1936 and money was hard to come by; it was especially difficult to come by if you were a Negro.

So Jesse Owens began to run for a living.

He went on tours with Negro baseball teams. He fronted for a dance band. He staged running exhibitions against motorcycles and race horses. He went all over the world running, running, running. He was married now, and children were coming along, and he had a family to support. He had to keep running.

As late as 1948, Jesse Owens was still running. His last race was held that year in Barcelona, Spain. He ran the 100 in 9.7s. and then he quit running.

He settled down with his family in Chicago. He did public relations work, he had his own radio show (where he was billed as "the world's fastest human disc jockey"). He went around the country making appearances at banquets. He was always in great demand.

He wore horn-rimmed glasses and conservative suits and he smoked a pipe and smiled at the world. His weight went up to 185 pounds and he became a grandfather, but he never lost his youthful look.

Jesse Owens' time is past, but it is time remembered. To the day he dies Jesse Owens will not have to worry about being forgotten. People, like the American boy and the Italian man at the Olympic Stadium in Rome in 1960 at the beginning of our story, remember still. People will always remember. Jesse Owens, to the day he dies, will always be able to walk like a king.

"I never went through a back door in my life," he once said. He never will have to.

Bill Tilden

TENNIS, a definition: "A defensive game played with an offensive attitude."

From Webster's New World Dictionary? No, sir. From William Tatum Tilden 2nd, the master tennis player of all time. It was a perfect definition of the

sport but it was a bit more than that. It was also an exquisite definition of Bill Tilden himself. For if anyone had the "offensive attitude" on and off the court, it was this tall, slim, hawk-faced man with the huge shoulders, trim waist, deep chest and indestructible legs.

For almost thirty years, Bill Tilden was the ruling

head of the sport. For ten of those years—from 1920 to 1930—he was almost unbeatable. In addition to being the greatest tennis player who ever lived, Bill Tilden may also have been the most arrogant.

One day while he was playing a match at Newport he stopped in the middle of a set to demand a cup of hot tea. Another time at the Forest Hills national championship, the tournament chairman refused Tilden's request to wear spiked shoes for a match. So Big Bill eased himself into a comfortable chair and stayed there. He was not going to move until he got permission to wear spikes. As 10,000 fans hollered and hooted and stomped their feet for the match to begin, Tilden sat unmovable.

Finally, a committeeman came over, glared at Big Bill, leaned down and cried, "This is preposterous."

"It certainly is," said Tilden, his long horseface lighting up in a bemused smile. "When will you boobs learn to stop meddling with things you know nothing about?"

A few minutes later Tilden went out and played— with spikes.

For all of his sixty years Bill Tilden was an arrogant man. But it was more, really, than just arrogance. He was a complex human being, once described by tennis queen Alice Marble as "that strange temperamental man whom nobody really knows." Nobody ever did truly get to know Bill Tilden the man, but everybody in the world in his years of glory got to know all about Bill Tilden the tennis player. He played everywhere in the world. On the tennis court he was the Beatles rolled into one. He was the king of the court.

In 1950 when he was fifty-seven years old, King William was voted by the Associated Press the tennis player of the half century. Out of 393 votes cast, Tilden received 310. Babe Ruth, who led in baseball, got only 253 votes. Jack Dempsey, the boxing leader, got only 251. Tilden was off by himself. You can argue for hours on end about who was the greatest player in baseball, in football, in boxing, in most other sports, and never come to any conclusion. But not in tennis. Don Budge, possibly the second best tennis player of all time, put it this way:

"Bill was the only genius tennis has produced. He stunned me so often, left me helpless on the court—many years after he was past his prime—that I'll believe anything they write about him."

It is all down in the books. The world's most important amateur championship is held at Wimbledon in England. Tilden became the first American to win the Wimbledon men's singles title. He took it a third time in 1930 when he was thirty-seven. In the United States he won thirty-one national amateur singles, doubles and mixed doubles championships. He won the U.S. singles championship seven times, six in succession, and he reached the finals all but twice from 1918 through 1929. Only one other man, Fred Perry, ever won the U.S. singles title as much as three times.

The United States never had a greater Davis Cup player. For eleven years he was a member of the U.S. Davis Cup team, in competition with teams from all over the world. From 1920 through 1926 the United States held the Davis Cup because of Tilden's mastery. In those years he won thirteen straight singles matches. And, remember, this was at a time when the world was full of first-class amateur tennis players.

Obviously, the man with the Gary Cooper build had everything. Listen to Allison Danzig, this country's finest tennis writer, on Tilden: "He had the greatest two-sided attack from the baseline the world has ever seen. They can talk about Don Budge's backhand and Ellsworth Vines' paralyzing forehand. Tilden was just as strong from either side.

"Big Bill could hit his shot back and straight down or across the court with the velocity of a bullet. He had one of the best cannonballs that ever belched aces, and his twist had a terrific kick. He was a master of spin without equal. He could beat you with flat speed from the back of the court or he could win by destroying your control with forehand chops and sliced backhand."

That was Bill Tilden the technician. But his game was built on much more than technique. In 1922, Franklin P. Adams wrote: "Tilden is an artist. He is more an artist than anything else, the tennis idealist who is more concerned with making a beautfiul shot or executing a bit of imaginative strategy than he is in actually winning a point. At a critical moment in a match he will try a fantastically difficult shot merely for the sheer joy he gets from producing this effect. It is the beauty of the game that Tilden loves—it is the chase always rather than the quarry."

And so it was. He never allowed himself the luxury of winning a match 6-0, 6-0, 6-0. If his opponent was a younger player, Bill would build up the youngster's confidence by allowing him to take a game or two, before crushing him. And Tilden was often at his most magnificent when he was behind. One day a ranking American player took the first set from Tilden and a friend of Bill's bet $500 that Tilden would win the next set, 6-1. Tilden heard about the bet and immediately lost the first game without trying. Then, with Tilden's friends sweating on the sidelines, Big Bill himself hardly worked up a sweat as he swept the next six games.

He played that way even in championship games. One day, Bill was playing René LaCoste of Paris. LaCoste was one of the famous French "Four Musketeers"—Jean Borotra, Henri Cochet, Jacques Brugnon were the others. The four Musketeers dominated international tennis from 1927 through 1932, winning the Davis Cup in each of those years. LaCoste was perhaps the best of them.

With 15,000 Frenchmen hollering for their "Crocodile," as they called LaCoste, the match went to a fifth set. The games were even when Bill played a backhand chop to LaCoste's forehand. Figuring that the Musketeer would hit a certain angled volley, Tilden raced to his forehand court. Just as he got there, LaCoste hit a beautiful shot. Bill leaped desperately, got his racquet on the ball outside the net post and between it and the umpire's chair. He flipped the ball as he went crashing into the concrete court rim and pinwheeled over into the crowd. Looking back upside down, Tilden saw LaCoste standing at the net, shaking his head. The ball had just cleared the cords and landed out of reach. That was too much for 15,000 Frenchmen and for René LaCoste. On his next serve he double-faulted and Tilden went on to run out the match.

That was in 1929 when Bill Tilden was thirty-six years old, which is very old for a tennis player. It was

1929, the year the stock market crashed, the year a depression was setting in on the country. The end of an era, the end of a decade.

Bill Tilden came along, with Dempsey and Ruth and Bobby Jones and Red Grange, to be part of the Golden Age of sports, the Golden Twenties, the most romantic sports period in our history. On the edge of that era, in 1919, Bill Tilden was already twenty-six years old, and a failure.

He was born on February 10, 1893, in the exclusive Germantown district of Philadelphia. Unlike most of the other sports heroes of his age, Bill Tilden never knew poverty. His father was a prosperous wool-and-hair merchant, a leading citizen of the Philadelphia area. His mother was a cultivated woman and an accomplished pianist. Tilden grew up, he admitted, "somewhat spoiled and a brat."

"My older brother, Herb, was the real tennis star of the family," Bill told writer Al Stump. "I was just 'Junior' Tilden, the pestiferous punk who got into the older kid's hair."

Herb Tilden was an excellent tennis player as a youngster. But Bill was coming along, too. He won his first title at age seven. At twelve and thirteen, he was a ballboy at the Germantown Cricket Club, where the world's leading amateurs played. But then his growth as a tennis player just seemed to stop. Between the ages of fifteen and twenty-five years, when most athletes develop and reach their peak, Tilden grew in size only. He grew a gangling 6 feet, 2 inches, but his tennis progress was nil. One old newspaper account of the day mentioned his "futility" as a tennis player.

Bill enrolled at the University of Pennsylvania

where he made the varsity tennis team and where his strange personality began to flourish. Part of it might have been caused by the death, in a six-year period, of his mother, father and brother. Nervous and high-strung, Bill quit college in his senior year and went to work for the Philadelphia *Ledger* as a drama and music reporter. Later he wrote sports.

Meanwhile, he continued to play tennis. In 1913 and 1914 he won his first national title, in mixed doubles with Mary Browne. But everyone felt that Mary Browne, the women's national singles champion, had "carried" Bill. In 1916 he appeared in his first national singles championship and lost to the junior champion, Harold Throckmorton. In 1918 Tilden became runner-up in the national singles and won the national doubles with a fifteen-year-old prodigy, Vinnie Richards. But the only reason he did so well, the critics felt, was because the good players were off to war. Tilden had tried to enlist but was rejected because of flat feet.

And now it was 1919 and the war was over and the great players were back and the greatest American player—William Johnston—smashed Tilden in straight sets in the U.S. singles final.

That humiliating defeat did something to Tilden. To a less resolute character it might have caused him to pack it in, to say, "Forget it; I can't make it." But not Bill Tilden. That defeat pricked at his immense pride. That defeat steeled him, reinforced his desire to become the best. But he knew he had to improve his game. His serve was not overpowering enough, his backhand was ineffective—Johnston had riddled it in their championship meeting. So Bill retired to Providence, Rhode Island, where he had a job with a life insurance company. He spent all his spare time perfecting his game. He remembered that period as a turning point in his life. He told writer Al Stump:

"I spent hours in serving alone, trying to disguise the twist and pace of the ball. I would take a dozen balls and serve them to No. 1 court with one style of delivery. Then I'd cross over and hit them back with another type of service. Next, I'd try the left court from both sides. My next move would be to pick out a certain section of the service court and aim for that until I could put the ball just where I wanted it. Finally, I'd strive to put the ball there with tremendous speed."

He also worked on his backhand, worked to make his backhand a flat smashing drive instead of a weak defensive slice. And he polished the rest of his game, too.

By the spring of 1920 he felt that now he was ready as he ever would be. And he set out to show the world.

Historians say the Golden Age of sports opened in 1920. The Golden Age of tennis opened in 1920, all right.

It opened quietly in New York at the beginning of the year on an indoor court. Bill Tilden beat Vinnie Richards for the national indoor singles title.

Then came the London championships and in the singles final it was Tilden against Bill Johnston, and once again Johnston was a winner. But Tilden was unworried. He was using the competition of a relatively minor tournament to sharpen his game. He was preparing for the biggest goal of them all—Wimbledon.

For forty-three years British Empire contestants

only had won at Wimbledon. But a revolution was coming. In an early round Tilden whipped J. C. Parke, who had eliminated Bill Johnston. Then he beat the No. 1 Englishman, Algy Kingscoate. Now the U.S. player was in the semi-finals against the defending champion, Gerald Patterson, the world's No. 1 player, representing Australasia.

The match started out in typical Tilden fashion, Patterson winning the first set easily, 6-2. In later years Tilden enjoyed exciting the gallery by letting his opponent take a dangerous lead and then, with the stage properly set and the crowd won over to Bill Tilden the underdog, staging a brilliant comeback to win. But this was different. This was London 1920 and Tilden was not yet established as the king and the British crowd would have none of that underdog stuff. Their hearts were securely with the Australian, a member of the British Empire. The king and queen of England sat in the royal box, fully expecting Patterson to prevail.

This expectation continued even when Tilden won the second set, 6-3. There was less cheering when he won the third set 6-2, and visible groans when he carried off the match, winning the fourth set, 6-4. The next day the London *Times* mourned, "Thousands had thought Patterson unbeatable. What happened in full view of their majesties will rank with such debacles as Hastings and Bunker Hill."

The Wimbledon final was anticlimactic. Tilden easily beat the little Japanese star, Zenzo Shimizu.

Tilden was immediately named to the Davis Cup team. Australasia (a combination of Australia and New Zealand) was the defending champion but first the Americans had to beat the French and the British. Big Bill Tilden and "Little Bill" Johnston, as he was now called, did just that. In the decisive doubles match against the British, Tilden was the sensation. In the fifth game of the fifth set, Tilden threw up a cannonball serve and J. C. Parke, a ten-second man in track, didn't get within two yards of the ball. The next serve by Tilden smashed into Algy Kingscoate's stomach, knocking him down. The third hurricane serve left Parke standing helplessly, his mouth open. "Such a thing had never been seen at Wimbledon before," said an eyewitness, "and the crowd did not know whether to cheer or regard it as a sacrilege."

The United States went on to meet Australasia in the Challenge Round and Bill Tilden beat Norman Brookes and Gerald Patterson in singles and then teamed with Little Bill Johnston to whip the Aussies and bring the Davis Cup back to America for the first time since 1913.

But Tilden had one more big goal that year, the U.S. championship. He wanted that very badly, and he knew one man stood in his way, Little Bill.

Bill Johnston stood only five feet eight and weighed a slight 120 pounds but he was a tremendous tennis player. He had won his first American title in 1915. He had a devastating forehand drive and a sound all-around game. In later years Tilden was to say about Johnston, "He was one of the most gallant souls I ever knew—the greatest fighting heart tennis ever had." But in the late summer of 1920, Tilden had no such gracious thoughts in his mind about Johnston. He wanted to beat Little Bill and so establish himself as the No. 1 American tennis player.

Over 10,000 spectators packed the Forest Hills stadium in New York to see the finals, Big Bill vs. Little Bill. It turned out to be one of the most dramatic matches ever played.

Tilden won the first set, 6-1. Johnston fought back savagely and won the second set by the same score. The third set started uneventfully, with Big Bill taking a 3-1 lead. Then, as Little Bill was about to serve, a small airplane carrying a cameraman and pilot flew in low over the field, so low that the crowd cried out in terror. Tailspinning, the plane crashed just outside the stadium. Both men died and the crowd became hysterical and threatened to stampede from the stands.

The tennis players were as badly shaken as the spectators. Neither knew what to do, but the umpire realized in a flash that the panic must be stopped and so he ordered play to resume. Tilden won the third set 7-5. In the fourth set he was within two points of the match when Johnston rallied and made a fantastic return of a smash at point-blank range. The crowd was working up to near-hysteria again.

Suddenly, the mood was heightened again when a driving rainstorm broke over the stadium. With a rally in progress, Tilden stopped play, mistakenly thinking that the umpire had called time. The point was awarded to Johnston, though against his wishes. The players rushed for shelter until the rain stopped and the court was cleaned up. Immediately, Tilden served three double faults and Johnston had the fourth set, 7-5.

The last set was played in half light, the long afternoon drawing to a close, but Big Bill never lost heart. His chopped undercut strokes bounced low on the wet court and his serve flashed ace after ace. Little Bill could not contain the fury of Big Bill and Tilden carried off the set, 6-3. He was now the champion of America as well as England.

In the clubhouse afterwards, Little Bill sat exhausted and raged. "Those legs. He beat me with those legs. But I'll get him next time. I'll get him—if it kills me."

It was not to be. In the next five years the great tennis rivalry in the world was Big Bill vs. Little Bill. In four of those years the two were finalists at Forest Hills. But never again was Little Bill able to beat Big Bill in a major match.

That was no disgrace. Those were the years of absolute majesty for Bill Tilden. In 1921 Tilden won the world hard court singles championship while suffering from fever and an attack of boils. He was called from a sickbed to defend his title against Brian I. C. Norton, the South African champion. Norton won the first two sets, 6-4, 6-2 and the crowd berated Tilden. "Play the game!" they cried. "Slacker." Tilden retaliated by winning the next three sets, then collapsed in the clubhouse in a dead faint.

He was still not fully recovered from his illness when he played in the Davis Cup Challenge Round against Zenzo Shimizu. Shimizu hardly came up to Big Bill's shoulders. He wore a flopping white hat and a perpetual childlike smile on his face. But he played tennis like a man twice the size. He went out and took the first two sets from Tilden, 7-5, 6-4.

Weary and sick, the heat beating into his body, Tilden managed somehow to win the third set. At the intermission Davis Cup captain Sam Hardy found Tilden standing, fully clothed, under the showers.

"Just dress me in dry clothes," Tilden grunted, "and push me out the door."

He made it back and swept the last two sets, 6-2, 6-1.

And his reign continued. He won everything in sight in 1922. In 1923 he won his third straight national singles cup, the U.S. Clay Court, mixed doubles and doubles titles. He was magnificent in Davis Cup competition as the U.S. ripped Australasia three years in a row.

In 1925 Bill Tilden was thirty-one years old and beginning to tire just a bit. Now the French were on the rise, the Four Musketeers.

In the Challenge Round of 1925, played at Germantown, Bill Tilden met Jean Borotra in the opening singles. Borotra won the first set, 6-4, Tilden won the second set, 6-0, Borotra won the third set, 6-2. Then Bill rallied to sweep the next two sets.

In his next singles match against René LaCoste, he was one point away from defeat. LaCoste had won the first set, 8-6, the second 12-10, and had command of the third set, until only one point separated him from a straight-set victory over the best tennis player in the world. At that point, Tilden smashed a forehand that was sure to go out of bounds by two feet. LaCoste had only to let the ball go. But in scrambling to get clear, he tripped and the ball hit the sole of his shoe. Tilden won the point, went on to sweep LaCoste.

He didn't need breaks like that very often, not this tall, slender man with the long loping stride, the fluent ground strokes from either side, the flashing chop and slice strokes, and the flat serve that came across the net like a shell. He was simply too much. But if he was too much to opponents, he was sometimes too much to tennis officials, to galleries, to the United States Lawn Tennis Association itself.

At times Tilden was unforgivable to umpires and linemen who made what he considered bad calls. Once when Sam Hardy, his old Davis Cup coach, called one against him, Tilden said, "You're blind, Sam—you didn't even see that ball." Other times when he felt a call had gone against him, he would stride to the line and point his racquet at the exact spot—according to Tilden—where the ball had struck. Then he would say, "Would you care to correct your error?" Sometimes they did.

This overbearing attitude earned him few fans. At the start of matches, the galleries would often cheer for Tilden's opponent; sometimes they booed Bill. That may be part of the reason that Tilden often began a match slowly and then staged a whirlwind come-from-behind victory. By the time he was down a set, most of the gallery was back rooting for him.

But the governing body of amateur tennis, the U.S.L.T.A. did little rooting for Bill Tilden. He continuously thumbed his nose at them, and got away with it. He accepted expense money far in excess of the rules. Once in the mid-twenties when he was asked why he didn't turn pro, he said, "Why, my dear fellow, I can't afford to."

He wrote a series of newspaper articles, which was also against amateur tennis rules. So what did the U.S.L.T.A. do? They turned around and changed the rules.

Just before a crucial Davis Cup match in Paris against the French, the U.S.L.T.A. announced they had suspended Tilden for writing a series of articles for a Philadelphia newspaper syndicate. The French, insisting on seeing Tilden play, raised such a stink that the suspension became a political issue. The American ambassador to France told the U.S.L.T.A. to reinstate Tilden. They did.

Tilden's popularity bobbed up and down like a cork in the water, but in one *losing* match in 1926, he had everyone with him. It happened in the U.S. singles championship when Tilden, hobbled by a chronic knee condition, lost a five-set war to Henri Cochet. Afterwards, one tennis reporter wrote, "Bill's star shines brighter than ever. Crippled, suffering agonies of body and mind, he almost plucked victory from certain defeat."

But now defeat was coming a bit more often. In 1927, in the Davis Cup Challenge Round, Bill Tilden gained revenge on Cochet with a four-set victory, but he was beaten by LaCoste, and the United States lost the Davis Cup for the first time in seven years.

And that was the end of one period of U.S. domination in tennis. Big Bill was getting old, Little Bill was getting old, the French Four Musketeers were on the rise.

Still, Tilden continued to hit high spots. His last year as an amateur, 1930, was one of his most amazing. Playing with a bad knee and a sacroiliac condition, Big Bill went to Europe and swept the Riviera tournaments. He won the national titles of Italy and Austria. Then, in his last great triumph, he beat Jean Borotra and Wilmer Allison at Wimbledon. And he became a three-time Wimbledon champion.

And then, age thirty-seven, he turned pro.

The immediate reason for the move was a movie

offer from MGM. For years Tilden had been an amateur actor. He loved to act. A tennis rival of Tilden's once said, "He was the consummate ham actor." So act he did. He played in two silent pictures and four tennis films and then he organized a professional tennis tour. He made his pro debut at Madison Square Garden on February 18, 1931, against the world pro champion, Karel Kozeluh of Czechoslovakia. Before 15,000 fans, Tilden won in straight sets.

In the next decade, Bill made good money playing pro tennis. At the age of forty-one he took on Ellsworth Vines, the reigning amateur champion who had just turned pro. Before 18,000 at New York's Madison Square Garden, he beat Vines in straight sets. One tour with Vines grossed $243,000. But his most memorable performance as a pro came in 1940 when he was forty-seven years old and about to play a match with the new king of tennis, Don Budge.

He was scheduled to play Budge before a sellout crowd in Edinburgh, Scotland. But a few days before the match, Tilden fell ill and was confined to the hospital with a high fever. On the day of the match he dragged himself out of bed and insisted on facing Budge.

"Let's wait until you're feeling better, Bill," said Budge. "I'd hate for you to look bad here."

Tilden's face set in grim lines. He looked right through Budge.

"I'll get the ball back to you," he said.

Budge took the court with mercy in his heart, determined to end the match as quickly as possible so as not to tax Tilden's strength. The match did end quickly, in one hour. Tilden beat Budge in straight sets.

The last years of Bill Tilden's life were not the happiest years. He was beset by personal problems. He drifted into obscurity, earning a living by coaching famous movie stars like Greta Garbo and Tallulah Bankhead. But he did continue to play tennis as often as he could. It was the one thing that made life worth living.

When he was fifty years old he could still beat anyone in the world in one set. Ten years earlier the critics had said, "Tilden needs new legs." But it was not true, it was never true. When he was fifty-seven, he rolled up his pant legs and showed writer Al Stump the underpinnings of a man twenty-five years younger.

"Does that look like the legs of an old man?" he asked triumphantly. "It's not the legs that go. It's something far more important than that. I played tennis at my best one time with a bum leg. I survived. The thing that gets an old man down is the unwillingness to take any more punishment. You just absolutely refuse to take another sock in the teeth. . . . That's the way it is with a tiring athlete. Whether it's his legs, back, eyes or anything else, doesn't matter much. The main concern is how long he can take it."

There was another concern, too. "The only thing I fear," Bill Tilden once said, "is being bored. When the capacity to enjoy life goes, it's time to die."

He died of a heart attack in June of 1953—alone in a hotel room. He was sixty years old and, presumably, it was time.

Maurice Richard

EVERY COUNTRY has its national hero. In the United States we have our John Glenn. In the Soviet Union, they have their Yuri Gagarin. Cuba has, if you'll pardon the expression, Fidel Castro. Sometimes, as when John F. Kennedy was President of the United States, the head of State is the national hero. But for eighteen years in the Dominion of Canada, especially among the French-speaking population, the national hero was a plain, ordinary athlete.

Ordinary did we say? We take that back. Joseph Henri Maurice Richard was super-extraordinary. Certainly the most remarkable hockey player of his time, some say he was the greatest hockey player of all time. If he wasn't the greatest, then certainly he was the most colorful, the most swashbuckling, the most daring, the most thrilling, the most commanding presence the sport of hockey has ever had. He was the Babe Ruth of hockey, an unbelievable crowd-pleaser, and for the French Canadians, who are a warm-blooded, excitable and passionate people, that was the standard of greatness. In every way, Maurice Richard lived up to that standard.

His tremendous appeal was compounded mainly of two basics: His ability for scoring goals, and the way

he fought back against his tormentors. Richard played in 1,978 National Hockey League games and spent 1,473 minutes of that time in the penalty box, a lifetime record second only to that of Ted Lindsay, the old badman of the Detroit Red Wings. For Maurice Richard, the penalties were seldom trivial. During his career, he paid out almost $3,000 in fines. He once sparked a riot in Montreal that caused $100,000 in damage, more than one hundred arrests and a forfeited game.

The reason was simple. Richard was a fiery, hot-tempered, unpredictable Frenchman. The way for an opposing team to ease the pressures that Richard put on them was to get him off the ice, to goad him into penalties. Dick Irvin, the coach of the Montreal Canadiens in Maurice's early years, once said: "Richard was the most illegally held, pushed, battered and elbowed man in the league. The did everything but send army tanks in to stop him. It was not unusual to see two defensemen, both bigger than he was, holding onto the sweater while an opposing wing tried to knock the puck off his stick."

There was only one thing for Richard to do—fight back. And fight back he did.

One day a New York Ranger defenseman with the appropriate nickname of "Killer" Dill was sent out to incite Richard. Dill did it in a very elementary way. He bumped Richard, then threw a straight right at Richard's head. Maurice ducked, and countered with a right of his own. The blow knocked Dill cold. Without waiting for a whistle, Richard calmly skated to the penalty box. When Dill regained consciousness he too was put in the penalty box.

As he moved in he saw Richard grinning at him. Enraged, he swung again. Again Maurice slipped the blow and shot out a left of his own. It caught Dill flush on the jaw and the Ranger enforcer was out for three more minutes.

But Maurice Richard was at his artistic best not at fighting but at scoring goals. Canadien coach Toe Blake, who partnered Richard on the great Punch Line of the late forties—Elmer Lach at center, Blake at left wing, Richard at right wing—said of Richard, "He lives for only one thing—to put that puck in the nets." And that was what most endeared him to his fellow French Canadians.

The thrill began in the crowd as soon as Richard (pronounced Ree—shar) swept onto the ice. At the beginning it was a low murmur, like a prayer whispered in church. Then, as Richard picked off the puck and began skating towards the enemy goal, his jet black hair streaming in the backwash of his hurtling assault, the murmur began to swell— a rising crescendo of taut cries. And when he let go and rocketed that flaming shot of his that could carry in at eighty miles an hour, the 15,000 spectators at the Montreal Forum became transformed into a mighty chorus singing a joyous hymn. Maurice "the Rocket" Richard had attacked again.

For eighteen years Richard struck that thrill in the hearts of his countrymen. For eighteen years he sped into goalies like a motorcar coming at them at night, his eyes gleaming like headlights. In that time he scored 544 goals, a lifetime figure second only to Gordie Howe of the Detroit Red Wings. In 133 playoff games he scored another eighty-two goals. Eighty of his goals won games for the Montreal Canadiens, eighteen of them won playoff games. He was the consummate clutch performer, always at his best under extreme pressure.

In the 1951 Stanley Cup semifinals against the favored Red Wings, Richard scored winning goals in three of Montreal's four victories, two of them in overtime. In the finals against Toronto, each of the five games went into overtime. The Canadiens won only one of those games. Richard scored a goal in each game and in the only Canadien victory it was Richard's sudden-death goal that did it.

Of all his brilliant clutch performances, perhaps the most astonishing came in the Stanley Cup semifinals against the Boston Bruins. Late in the second period, in the game that would decide it all, the score was tied, 1-1. Swirling down the ice, Richard bounced off Bruin defenseman Leo Labine and crashed head first to the ice. He was carried unconscious to the dressing room, blood streaming from a gaping cut over his left eye. He remained unconscious as the doctor put six stitches in his forehead and swabbed his cheek. He came around slowly and midway in the third period, still groggy, he was sent back to the Canadiens' bench.

He was half out of the world but the Rocket was aware of one thing—on the ice a war was still going on. With the score still tied and only four minutes left, Richard appealed to his coach, Dick Irvin.

"Let me out there," he begged. "Let me play."

Irvin looked at Richard, hesitated, then said, "Okay, get in for this faceoff."

The man moved into action right away. He took a pass from defenseman Butch Bouchard in the Montreal zone and sped towards the enemy. Woody Dumart stuck out his stick. Richard bounced the puck over it, sidestepped Dumart, and regained control of the puck in the center zone. Waiting for him were Bob Armstrong and Bill Quackenbush, two tough Bruin defenders.

For a moment, Quackenbush pinned Richard to the boards. The Rocket, his forehead bleeding again, twisted away from Armstrong, still holding the puck. Quackenbush came up to meet Richard but Rocket put on a burst of speed, drove by Quackenbush and cut towards the center ice to the front of the net. Then he fired.

He heard yells but he didn't know what had happened. He didn't know until his teammates came over and started hugging him and slapping him on the back. Maurice Richard had scored the winning goal.

There is a photo of that game that tells all about Maurice Richard. It shows the Bruins' goalie Sugar Henry shaking hands with Richard. There is a tape over the Rocket's left eye and a thin line running down his face onto his neck. His eyes are the eyes of a puzzled man, the eyes almost of a hypnotized man. But the lips—the lips—are set firm and triumphant. In the dressing room after that victory a teammate came over to Richard and said, "You play better when you are unconscious." At that, Richard sat on the rubbing table and started to cry. He cried until his father came in and talked to him and calmed him down.

This was Maurice Richard, proud, emotional, able to unfold his magic even without full possession of himself. "Maurice's moves," said Canadiens' managing director Frank Selke, "were powered by instinctive reflexes. He did everything by instinct and sheer power."

That wasn't the sum of it, however. The sum and substance of Maurice Richard was that hockey was his heart and soul—"the most urgent thing in my life," as he once said.

It was that way even when he was a child skating on the Black River near his home. He was born on August 4, 1921, in a tenement in the northeast end of Montreal. His father, Onesime, was a semipro baseball player who worked for the Canadian-Pacific railroad. Eight kids were born to Onesime and Alice Richard and it was a hard life. But hockey was a way out for Maurice.

The snows were severe when Maurice was growing up. The snow would come early and then be packed down and the children would skate to school on top of it. Maurice was four years old when he began to ice skate. Soon he began to play hockey, began to play with that urgency which was to characterize his whole career. He would come home from school and go right out and play till 5:30 in the evening. Many times he would keep his skates on while he ate and then go out and play more hockey after supper.

When he finished the ninth grade he went to the École Technique in downtown Montreal, studying to be a machinist. He played for his school team and any other teams that would have him in the area.

When he was eighteen he played for the Verdun Juniors in the Quebec Junior Hockey League. He was a dark, somber-looking young man. He spoke no English and he was uncommunicative. He didn't excite as a hockey player, either. He was five feet ten inches, weighed 160 pounds and his talents seemed ordinary. He didn't get to play much but the next year he did make the jump to the Canadiens' Senior team in the Quebec Senior Hockey League. In his first game, on one of his first turns on the ice, he collided with a Quebec Aces' player and snapped his right ankle. He was out the rest of the year.

The next year was almost as bad. He reported to the Canadiens' Seniors again, played only a few games and broke his left wrist. Still, the Canadiens liked the reports they had received on the young Canadian and he was invited to the pro Canadien camp in 1942.

Kenny Reardon, a star defenseman for the Canadiens for many years and later an executive with the club, remembered Richard as "looking like a mangy bear. He had all this hair on him," Reardon said. "If he had another hair on his back, he'd be up a tree."

But on the ice it was different. Reardon remembers his first contact with Richard. "I see this guy skating at me with wild, bloody hair the way he had it then, eyes just outside the nuthouse. 'I'll take this guy,' I said to myself. He went around me like a barrel."

Richard had an excellent training period and Dick Irvin, the coach of the Canadiens, was anxious to sign him. But Richard balked. He wanted a two-year contract. Finally, just before the start of the season, Irvin gave in. That contract was a break for Maurice. He played fifteen games with the Canadiens, scored five goals and six assists. But in his next game against the Bruins, he walked into a hard check tossed by defenseman Johnny Crawford. Off balance, he fell and the skate tip lodged in a piece of soft ice. He snapped his right ankle and he was through for the year.

Now the Canadiens' management was bitten by doubts. Irvin told Richard, "You're too brittle, kid." But Richard had that two-year contract and so the Canadiens had to give him another opportunity.

Maurice came back in 1943 and he showed them. He was put on the line with Lach and Blake. That season it became known as the Punch Line and the Punch Line it was. With the Punch Line leading the way, the Canadiens won the league championship and scored their first Stanley Cup victory in twelve years. And in the playoff, Richard was magnificent. He scored twelve goals in nine games, a playoff record. In one game against Toronto, he scored all five goals.

The next year it was better. The Canadiens swept to another league championship and Maurice Richard, with arms and legs of steel plus his indomitable fighting spirit, was at his height. In one game, on December

28, 1944, he came into the Canadiens' dressing room and said, "Don't depend on me too much. Today I helped my brother to move. We could get no truck and I carried nearly everything on my back. I'm so tired."

All he did in that game was score five goals and three assists, a single-game record at the time.

In all that season, Richard scored seventy-three points. And his fifty goals was a new record, a record that has not been broken to this day. Boom Boom Geoffrion and Bobby Hull both tied the fifty-goal record, but both men did it in a seventy-game schedule. Richard set his in a fifty-game season.

And the goals he was making! In the 1945-46 season he was streaking in toward the net, with only Earl Siebert, Detroit's 225-pound defenseman to beat. Instead of trying to sidestep Siebert, Maurice bent his head and busted right into the burly, unsuspecting Siebert. The collision rocked the arena and cracked the ice. Siebert was literally on Richard's back. The Rocket straightened up, still managing to control the puck, and carried Siebert on his back. He carried him toward the net, faked the goalie out of position with his free hand and slammed the puck into the far corner. When Siebert came back to the bench, crestfallen, Detroit coach Jack Adams was livid. "Why, you big dummy," he said.

"Listen, Coach," interrupted Siebert. "Any guy who can carry me sixty feet and then put the puck into the net—well more power to him."

But now World War II was over and Maurice Richard would be truly tested. "At that time," said Frank Selke, "he was thought of as a wartime player.

When the boys came back they said they'll look after Maurice. They said, they'll catch up with him."

The war veterans found out. In the 1946-47 season, the Canadiens won another league championship and Richard led the league with forty-five goals. In the playoffs he led all scorers with six goals and eleven total points. Montreal lost to Toronto in the playoff but Richard had established himself. He was the real thing. He won the Hart trophy as the National Hockey League's most valuable player. And he also showed the returning veterans a little bit of the explosive Richard temper.

It came in the playoffs against Toronto. As usual, the Rocket was tightly guarded at all times. As usual, he was held, pulled and spilled. In one center-ice collision he was spilled by Vic Lynn. He lashed out at Lynn with his stick, catching Lynn in the left eye. He spent the next five minutes in the penalty box. But his big explosion was yet to come.

Wild Bill Ezinicki, the Toronto defenseman, was the Rocket's chief antagonist. Ezinicki stayed with Richard like he was his Siamese twin. Finally, the Rocket skated back to the bench for a rest and Irvin leaned over to him and said, "That guy will never get off your back if you don't show him who's boss."

Maurice just nodded to Irvin. When he went back on ice he caught up with Ezinicki as Wild Bill came across from behind his net. He piled right into Ezinicki. He swung once and knocked Ezinicki cold. The Rocket was tossed out of the game and drew a $250 fine and suspension. But he was happy. "Ezinicki," he said with satisfaction, "was never quite as free with his hands around me again."

There was no particular secret to Richard's marvelous skills on the ice. "If there is any secret at all about scoring goals," Rocket once said, "it is the ability to get clear for a shot. I wasn't the fastest nor the most powerful skater in the league. I tried to combine what speed I had with the strength to bull my way past enemy defenses."

Richard skated with a long stride, his feet wide apart. Instead of playing the puck from side to side to elude checks, he kept it in one position and depended mostly on power. Frankie Brimsek, the great Boston Bruins' goalie, the Mr. Zero of the Bruins, once tried to analyze Richard's style:

"He can shoot from any angle," said Brimsek. "You play him for a shot to the upper corner of the net because his stride, his grip on the stick and everything else indicates that's where he's going to shoot. So you cover that part of the net. Almost anticipating your move, Richard wheels around and fires a backhander into the near, lower part of the net."

Instinct, the magic of sheer instinct. Throughout one game, for instance, the Rocket was closely guarded by Tony Leswick of the New York Rangers. He grabbed a loose puck and drove for the net. He was inside the Rangers' blue line set for the shot when Leswick grabbed him by the sweater, jabbed a stick into his ribs and pushed him into Gus Kyle, a big defenseman. Kyle smashed the Rocket to the ice and fell on top of him. Leswick piled on as the puck slid away. But the Rocket wasn't through. Somehow, he got his stick on the disc, feinted goalie Chuck Raynor out of position with a quick thrust, and rammed the puck into an empty corner of the cage.

Such miracle goals happened many times when Rocket Richard was on the ice. Red Hammill, who played defense for the Chicago Black Hawks, recalled a game when Richard came bearing down on Hammill. "I couldn't catch him against the boards," Hammill said, "so I let him move inside my position. The other defenseman moved over and we thought we had him good. We both body-checked hard. He bounced from one to the other like a yo-yo and fell to the ice. But while he was falling he reached out and lashed at the loose puck. When I looked around, there was the puck in the rigging and the goal light was blinking in my face."

Season after season, Maurice worked his magic on the ice, without a let-up. In 1952, he scored his 325th goal, breaking the career record of Nels Stewart. And on and on he went.

Fans from every city in the NHL flocked to Canadien games, not so much to root for their own home team, not so much to root against the Canadiens, but mostly to see the unpredictable Richard in action. What would he do next? The hat-trick perhaps? Three goals? Or would he turn around and just break his stick over someone's head? If the customers were lucky, Richard did both.

The customers were very lucky the night Richard tangled with the Detroit Red Wing team. It started when Ted Lindsay was given instructions: get on Richard, get him to commit a penalty, get him off the ice. Lindsay obliged and badgered Richard unmercifully. Finally, the Frenchman could take it no longer. He seemed to be trying to commit murder on Lindsay. The Red Wing defenseman escaped but not Richard.

He was hit with a five-minute major and a two-minute minor penalty. He watched in frustration as the Red Wings took a 2-0 lead.

When he had served his time he leaped onto the ice, grabbed a loose puck, infiltrated the defense and blazed a shot through the goal.

At the next face-off Elmer Lach grabbed the puck, passed it to Richard and the Rocket drilled a short backhand shot into the goal.

He was not through. Ignoring Dick Irvin's protests to get off the ice, the Rocket took the puck from Toe Blake on a face-off, feinted two defenders out of position, bowled right through Ted Lindsay and blasted a long shot high into the net. In three minutes the Rocket had scored three goals. The final score was 3-2, a Canadiens' victory.

But not all of Richard's close-order drills with the enemy ended so happily. In 1951 in a close game against the Canadiens, Richard was wrestled down by the Detroit center but referee Hugh McLean called no infraction. Richard was livid and argued mouth-to-mouth with the referee. For this he got a ten-minute misconduct penalty. That night Richard was unable to sleep. All he could think of was the injustice of it all.

The next morning he bumped into referee McLean in the lobby of a New York hotel. Without ceremony he grabbed for McLean's throat. Several of Richard's teammates had to pull him off the referee. The Rocket was fined $500 for "conduct prejudicial to the welfare of hockey."

Then, in 1955, Richard reached the absolute low point of his career. It was late spring. The Canadiens had four games to go and seemed about to break the

Red Wings' hold on the championship. Detroit had won six league titles in a row and, in the process, the Rocket had taken a bit of a backseat to the Red Wings' right wing, Gordie Howe. Howe was making first All-Star team and Richard second. But it looked different in '55 as the season drew to its close. The Canadiens held on to first place and Rocket held the league lead in scoring. The team went to Boston for a critical game, and Rocket, once more, got in trouble.

Hal Laycoe, the Boston defenseman, had grabbed the puck after a face-off. Richard chased after him. Trying to get the puck free, Richard jammed his stick into Laycoe's face. Laycoe turned and swung his stick at Richard, opening a gash on the side of his head.

The Rocket went berserk. He lunged at Laycoe, felt a restraining arm on his neck and, without looking, threw a punch at his tormentor. It was a lineman, Cliff Thompson. Thompson filed the report to the league office and Clarence Campbell, the president of the National Hockey League, took stern action. He banned Richard from the Canadiens' last three league games and *all* of the Stanley Cup games.

That set off a wild chain of events. Canadien fans, the French-speaking residents of Montreal who regarded Maurice Richard as a god, were incensed. Campbell was besieged by anonymous phone calls threatening his life. As it happened the Canadiens' next home game was against Detroit and Campbell, brave but imprudent, said he would attend.

He arrived midway in the first period with the Canadiens losing and that was all the Canadien fans needed. More than two hundred policemen inside the arena were unable to maintain order. There was a shower of eggs, peanuts, programs, even overshoes. A fan came over and slugged Campbell and then a smoke bomb exploded. Campbell immediately awarded the game to the Red Wings on a forfeit and the rioting spilled out onto the street.

It was an ugly riot as all riots are, one of the worst riots in Montreal's history. Automobiles were overturned, passing streetcars were stoned, store windows were smashed. There was looting. More than one hundred people were arrested with damage totalling more than $100,000. Finally, Maurice Richard had to take the air.

Speaking over the radio in French, then English, Richard pleaded for calm, for a return to order. "I will take my punishment," he said, "and come back next year to help the younger players to win the Cup."

He was true to his word. The next five years were the glory years for the Canadiens. With such youngsters as Jean Beliveau, Dickie Moore, Boom Boom Geoffrion, Jacques Plante and Richard's younger brother, Henri, the Canadiens were supreme again. They won four out of five league championships. They won five straight Stanley Cups. And Maurice Richard continued to be the catalyst, the big man. Refusing to grow old, Richard played the inspired hockey of a man fifteen years younger. He had gotten heavier (he weighed 185 pounds in those days) and he could not skate as fast as he once could, but he still had that frightening shot. And he still had that unquenchable fighting spirit.

He was thirty-six years old when he had perhaps the finest moments of his hockey career.

The 1957-58 season began in gloom for Richard. On

November 22, 1957, the night the Canadiens were to meet the Toronto Maple Leafs, Rocket was leading the league in scoring. Early in the game he cut into center ice and was about fifteen feet inside the Toronto blue line. He took a shot and as he did so he fell forward on the ice. Toronto defenseman Marc Reaume was in front of the Rocket, his back to him. Maurice slid into Reaume from behind and Reaume fell backward onto the Rocket. Richard felt a sudden stab of pain as he tried to get up. Reaume's left skate had cut deep into Rocket's achilles tendon. The tendon was cut almost two-thirds of the way through.

For the next thirty-six days Richard wore a plaster cast that extended from his toes to six inches above his knees. Nobody knew whether he would be able to play hockey again. After two months Richard got back on skates and tried out the foot. But it was no good. He found he could not skate without great pain. He thought gravely about his future.

Late in February, tormented by inner doubts, Richard determined to try again. Either he could play again or he could not. He went out on the ice and discovered that the pain in his heel was not as intense when he skated as when he walked. On February 20 he played his first game in over three months. He scored two goals. He scored two more the next night. He felt like the Rocket of old.

The proud Canadien team won its third straight league championship. In the semifinal playoff against Detroit, the Canadiens swept the first three games. The fourth game was played in Detroit and the script seemed to have changed. With twenty minutes left to play, the Red Wings led 3-1. Then Richard went to work. He scored three goals in a row, the hat trick, and the Canadiens beat the Wings, 4-3.

The Canadiens faced the Boston Bruins in the Stanely Cup finals. The teams split the first four games. The fifth game was just as close. At the end of regulation time, the score was tied, 2-2.

During the intermission, Frank Selke, the Canadiens' managing director, appeared on television. The announcer said, "Are you uneasy about the outcome of the game?"

"I'm not worried," Selke said. "We have Maurice Richard to decide this for us."

Maurice Richard decided, all right. He won the game with a sudden-death goal. And the Canadiens went on to win the sixth and deciding game. All Richard had done in this Stanley Cup, all this old man had done, was score eleven goals, just one short of his own record.

He went on for two more seasons, playing intermittently near the end. He had begun his career with three crippling injuries. He was ending his career the same way. During the 1958 season he broke his leg. In the 1959-60 season he fractured a cheekbone.

He gave it one more try in the training camp of the Canadiens in November 1960. He was over thirty-eight years old and he found that the game was now too fast for him. Sadly, he called a press conference and announced his retirement.

Things have never been the same in Montreal— never quite the same without the Rocket. Late in the fall of 1960 the Canadiens weren't doing too well and coach Toe Blake had one explanation.

"We miss the Rocket," Blake said. "The other team would be so busy covering Rocket we'd be able to break through and score before they knew what had happened. And the players looked up to him."

And this final epitaph from Toe Blake, who once skated with Maurice Richard on the Punch Line:

"It was always good when he was there."

Babe Didrikson Zaharias

Nature has given horns to bulls, hoofs to horses, swiftness to hares, the power of swimming to fishes, of flying to birds, understanding to men. She had nothing more for women.

NOT QUITE TRUE. That flash of wisdom was written in 500 B.C., approximately 2,000 years before a woman named Mildred Didrikson Zaharias was proving decisively that it was not necessarily a man's world.

For in 1950 Babe Didrikson Zaharias had just been voted the greatest woman athlete of the first half of the twentieth century. And no one in the world even came close.

She *was* the greatest.

She tried and mastered nearly all the games of the sporting world.

She played basketball so well that three times she

was chosen to play on the All-American women's basketball team.

In 1932 she won the national women's track and field championship. She scored thirty points all by herself. The runnerup, the Illinois Women's Athletic Club, had twenty-two contestants.

In the 1932 Olympics she qualified for five events, was allowed to compete in three. She set a new world's record for the hurdles. She threw the javelin farther than any woman had ever thrown it. She tied for first place in the high jump, another world's record.

She was a star in baseball. She once pitched a doubleheader against a girl's team. The Babe came to bat thirteen times. She hit nine home runs, two triples and a double, and drove in twenty-two runs. She was so good that she once pitched in an exhibition baseball game for the St. Louis Cardinals.

She played tennis for fun, but was good enough to take sets from such leading players as Louise Brough, Pauline Betz and Mary Arnold.

She was an excellent swimmer, diver, marksman, cyclist and figure skater.

She was a super bowler. In one three-game series, she bowled scores of 268, 234 and 214.

And then she took up golf and no woman in the world (and few men, either) could come close to her.

At 140 pounds, she could still power a golf ball an average of 230 yards, and sometimes she hit over 300 yards. She won fifty-five major tournaments in her fifteen years and she earned more money than any woman athlete had ever earned before.

Recovered temporarily from a grave cancer opera-

tion, the Babe went out and won the U.S. Open. She shot rounds of 72, 71, 73, 75. Par on that course was 72, for men.

Later that year she won the All-American, with a ten-under par 294. That was when she was weak, when she was dying.

She did it all, Babe Didrikson Zaharias did, and she was a woman.

She was not a beautiful woman, although a sports-writer, Westbrook Pegler, who admired her very much, did call her beautiful. He once wrote, "Babe probably did not realize it but she was a beautiful woman—from the mouth down. I certainly do not mean to be unkind in saying this because I did admire the girl for qualities apart from her skill in all sports. They were determination, courage, honesty and a candid but not immodest appreciation of her own superiority. Her body was slender but shapely and her legs were beautiful."

She was not beautiful but, as Pegler implied, she did have the quality of beauty. Much of it was inner beauty and it came out of the woman herself.

Mildred Didrikson was born in Beaumont, Texas, of Norwegian parents, on June 26, 1914. Ole Didrikson was a cabinetmaker and ex-seaman who had settled in Beaumont just after the turn of the century. Hanna Marie Olson Didrikson was from Oslo, Norway, where she had won ice skating contests.

There were seven children in the Didrikson family, three boys and four girls. Mildred was the sixth child. When she was small her brothers and sisters called Mildred "baby." Then, when Mildred was no longer a baby, her mother told the other children, "Mildred's getting to be a big girl now; it's about time you were calling her something else." So it became "Babe," and when she started playing baseball and started hitting the ball like a man named Babe Ruth, the nickname Babe stuck.

At Beaumont High School, the first sport she ex-celled in was basketball. She had tried out for the high school team as a five-foot 90-pound sophomore, but was told she was too small; so she practiced by the hour, barefoot, to perfect her two-handed set shot.

She made the team as a junior, and that was when this wiry little girl with the close-cropped hair and "door-step jaw" began to make a name for herself.

It was while she was playing basketball in Dallas in 1930 that a Colonel M.J. McComb spotted her. McComb's hobby was coaching a girl's athletic club and he immediately saw that Babe was a natural.

"Do you like other sports?" McComb asked the Babe.

"I like all sports," the Babe said.

"Are you as good at other sports as you are at basketball?" McComb asked.

The Babe smiled through her thin lips. "Try me out," she said.

McComb did, and was convinced.

At a track meet in Dallas one summer day that year, Babe saw a javelin lying on the ground. She picked it up. Somebody showed her how to hold it. She reared back and let it go.

"I broke the world's record on that throw," she remembered later. "The next year," she said, "I had only three days' practice hurdling before I broke the world's record. In a meet in New Orleans, I turned around and waited for the other hurdlers to come in."

So Babe moved to Dallas, took a job McComb's got for her as a $75-a-month typist for Employers Casualty Company and played basketball. One game she scored 100 points. The Golden Cycles, as McComb's team was called, won the Amateur Athletic Union championship in 1931. Babe was named to the girls' All-America team.

But there was an Olympics coming up in 1932, in Los Angeles, and so McComb organized a track team—and Babe was it.

"What events do you want to compete in?" McComb asked Babe.

"How many do they have in a track meet?" she asked.

"Oh, eight or nine."

"I'll try 'em all," Babe said.

She began working out seriously for the Olympics. She didn't have much time for the average girl's activities like dancing and dates. She had one thing on her mind—winning. "I never just wanted to be as good as anyone else," she once said, "I always wanted to be better."

It was at the national AAU championship in Evanston, Illinois, that Babe first shook up the world. Fifteen to twenty-two girls were gathered from various clubs. Babe alone represented the McCombs A.C.

She won the shotput, javelin throw, broad jump, baseball throw and 80-meter hurdles. She tied for first place in the high jump, scored a fourth in the discus throw, and failed to place in the 100-meter sprint. Her thirty points were enough for the team championship.

And two weeks later she was in Los Angeles for the Olympic games.

She had just turned eighteen, she stood five feet four inches tall, she weighed 110 pounds, she had green eyes and short sandy hair; she was built like a boy and she looked like a tomboy.

And she competed in the Olympic games like a man.

The hardest part of the Olympics for Babe Didrikson was the opening day ceremonies because she had to wear heels and stockings, part of the uniform of the girls' team. In the middle of the program she slipped off her shoes and happily wriggled her toes in the grass.

The next day she was comfortable again in sweat socks and spiked shoes.

Under a special Olympic rule, Babe was permitted to enter only three events. She chose the javelin, the hurdles and the high jump.

"Ah'm gonna whup you," she told her foreign rivals, emphasizing her Texas drawl. She was full of confidence.

That first day she won the javelin throw even though "it slee-upped" from her hand. She won it with a throw of 143 feet, 4 inches—a world's record for women.

On the fifth day of competition she won the 80-meter hurdles in 11.7 seconds, a world's record. Afterward she was sad. "I've got only one more event to break a record in," she said. "I'd break 'em all if they'd let me."

She almost did. In the high jump she broke another world's record, but this time she didn't win the gold medal. Babe and a teammate, Jean Shiley, tied at the height of 5 feet, 5¼ inches. In the jump-off, at the same height, both girls cleared the barrier but the Babe was disqualified for "diving." In those days, the rule was that the feet had to go over the bar first. So Babe had to settle for a silver medal.

They gave her a roaring reception when she returned in triumph to Dallas. She rode through the street in the Fire Chief's car and then she made a speech.

She said: "What I would like to do most is stay home here, get back on my job, start seriously on golf and help the Cycles win back the national basketball championship."

Soon, golf was to be her game.

She started playing golf in Dallas in 1930. One day her coach, Colonel McComb, was driving her home from basketball practice. McComb stopped at a driving range to hit some balls. The Babe sat in the car and watched. She watched in fascination. Soon, she was out of the car and buying a bucket of balls for herself. She swung at the first golf ball in her life. It was an awkward swing, but it was a man's swing. The swing turned her all the way around, and she broke the club on the post. The ball? It flew a straight 264 yards.

And the bug had bitten deep. In her spare time, when she was away from her typist's job, the basketball court, and running practice, she would go to a nearby golf course and work on her game. She practiced until her hands bled. She shot ten to fourteen hours daily. She hit thousands of golf balls a day.

But golf would have to wait for awhile. After the Olympics, after Babe Didrikson had been voted woman athlete of the year by the Associated Press, the Babe had become a celebrity. She decided to make some money on her name.

She wrote syndicated articles, she toured with a softball team, she was the only girl on the Babe Didrikson All-America basketball team. She played baseball with men, too—with the House of David, a group of talented ballplayers who all wore beards. She even went into vaudeville. She played a week at the Palace Theatre in New York. She cracked jokes, sang a song—"I'm Fit as a Fiddle and Ready for Love"—hit imaginary golf balls, ran around and played the harmonica.

In 1934 in an exhibition game in Florida, the Babe pitched an inning for the St. Louis Cardinals against the Philadelphia Athletics. It was a mixed success. The A's loaded the bases on three hits, but a double play got her out of trouble. Then Jimmy Foxx belted a long drive towards the trees in center, except that Paul Dean, getting a workout in the outfield, caught the ball. A three-out inning for the Babe and that was her major-league career.

By the end of 1934, the Babe had grown tired of running around the country cashing in on her reputation. She had made some $30,000 and now she could afford to take up golf seriously.

She entered her first tournament in Fort Worth, shot a 77, and won it.

In 1935 she won the Texas women's championship at the River Oaks Club, beating an experienced amateur, Peggy Chandler, two-up in the final round. She thought she was ready to go, but there was a problem.

It seems that the other ladies of the United States Golf Association—cowed by the Babe's phenomenal play—had complained about Babe Didrikson's amateurism. The complaint was upheld. Babe was declared ineligible, "for the best interest of the game."

Babe swallowed her disappointment, turned pro and toured the country with Gene Sarazen playing a series of exhibition golf matches.

In January of 1938 Babe was paired in the opening round of the Los Angeles Open with, of all things a 300-pound wrestler. His real name was Theodore

Veoyanis; his professional name was George Zaharias. The wrestler wasn't happy over the pairing arrangement either. He had hoped for a big name pro who would attract a large gallery. But when he shook hands with Babe, something happened. "A big thrill went through me," he remembered. "In a minute I had my arms around her, showing her wrestling holds for the photographers." In the middle of the round, surrounded by photographers, George turned to Babe.

"You're my kind of girl."

They had their first date that night. Eleven months later, they were married.

Babe Didrikson Zaharias now settled down, determined to be reinstated as an amatuer. In order to regain her amateur standing, she would have to shun all money from golf for three years. Babe served her three years well by sharpening her game while her husband earned the family living by wrestling. In 1944 she was fully reinstated as a golfer.

And then came the remarkable surge that was to make Babe Didrikson Zaharias the greatest woman golfer who ever lived.

Her game was based essentially on power, and what power she had for a woman! She once hit a ball 348 yards, including the roll. In Mexico City, aided by a gale wind, one of her tee shots went an impossible 422 yards. "I meant to hit the ball instead of swinging at it," and hit it she did. But there were other refinements to her game.

She always played fast, and straight. She was a sound strategist. She was a good putter though there were better women putters. Best of all, she had the killer instinct—the will to win. In her autobiography, "This

Life I've Led," Babe summed up her philosophy about sports this way:

"Before I was even into my teens, I knew exactly what I wanted to be when I grew up. My goal was to be the greatest athlete that ever lived."

Soon she was fulfilling her philosophy on the golf course.

In 1945 she swept everything in the way and was voted woman athlete of the year for the second time, and this time for a different sport, golf rather than track and field. In the 1946-47 season, Babe won nineteen straight tournaments. Her biggest tournament win that year was the British women's golf championship, played in Scotland. No American had ever won it before. Babe won it, 5 and 4 in the final round.

As soon as she had holed out, Babe put on kilts and did a Highland Fling, sang a Highland ditty and was swamped by wellwishers anxious to congratulate her and looking for autographs. It was two hours after her victory before she was able to reach the clubhouse. Everybody wanted to shake her hand or get an autograph. "It was the biggest thrill of my life," she said later.

In 1946 and '47 she was again named best woman athlete of the year.

Then, in 1948, aided by her husband, and a promoter, George May, she organized a ladies' pro tour.

There had been women pro golfers before Babe but they barely made a living. The ladies needed a name. They got a name. The tour was built around Babe Didrikson Zaharias and this time women's professional golf made it.

In 1951 Babe earned $15,087 in golf winnings, the

highest ever among professional women. And, for the fifth time, she was named woman athlete of the year.

Triumph succeeded triumph. And the scene was almost always the same. Babe Didrikson Zaharias storming the golf course, her husband puffing along beside her, offering his encouragement, acting as her agent, shielding Babe from the distractions that might hurt her golf game—and kissing her on the cheek for the photographers after she had won another one.

The Babe was in her prime. No longer was she a tomboy. She was a woman, a married woman of grace and charm. She wore tailored suits and carried initialed handbags and wore her hair in current styles, and her features were considerably softened.

She was at her peak, and it seemed that nothing could stop her. But in 1952 she had to go to the hospital for a hernia operation. Less than a year later she was back in the hospital. This time the diagnosis was severe—cancer.

The news became public and even before Babe entered the operating room she was flooded with letters and messages—15,000 of them. They all said about the same thing—"We're praying for you."

The operation seemed to be a success though Babe's doctor warned her that she might never play golf again. Three months later she was playing golf again.

When it came time to enter the All-American at Tam 'O Shanter, few people thought that Babe Zaharias would be well enough to compete. Her husband was one of them.

"Take your time, honey," George said. "There are plenty of other tournaments."

Babe was adamant. "I've got to find out right away if I can still play tournament golf."

"Of course you can," George said.

Babe smiled a wan smile. "It's the biggest thing in my life, George, next to you."

So Babe entered the All-American and her husband told newspaper-men, "I hope she can walk eighteen."

She could. She walked eighteen a winner in eighty-two strokes. That winter she was awarded the Ben Hogan trophy for the greatest comeback of the year.

She returned to the tournament trail, but on a selective basis. She still hadn't fully regained her strength. In 1954 she entered the U.S. Women's Open at the Salem Country Club in Peabody, Mass. The spectators stormed out to see the Babe, the largest crowd ever to watch women's golf. And they went home fulfilled.

On the 6,393-yard course, Babe's 291 was twelve strokes ahead of her nearest competitor.

Elated, she threw herself into her husband's arms. "This will tell the people not to be afraid of cancer," she said. "I'll go on golfing for another twenty years."

It was not to be. Soon after, she was back in the hospital. The cancer had struck again, had spread. Babe Didrikson Zaharias, who had dazzled the public as much as any of the great male sports heroes of the day, was doomed.

"Let's set our house in order," she told her husband. And they did. The Babe was in and out of the hospital. When out, she talked about playing golf again. When in, she read the daily bulletins about her illness.

"Let me read the papers to see how I feel today," she joked.

She held her head high as always, a fighter to the very last. The end came in 1956, but she had left a firm legacy behind her.

Willie Mays

THE Willie Mays cult among grown men is considerable and fervid in New York City. Willie Mays is champ with these gentlemen. Willie Mays is Superman, Batman, Captain Marvel, the Green Hornet—all bunched into one very big muscle. Willie Mays can do no wrong.

It would take pages to explain the reason for this hysterical worship among New Yorkers who are otherwise considered among the most sophisticated animals in the world. In my own case it was coming to New York to live and work in 1951 at the same time as Willie Mays was coming up to the New York Giants. So Mays and I grew up together and it didn't matter that he moved out of town to San Franscisco. It meant nothing. Willie Mays was as big as ever, maybe even more so now that he was no longer present.

I am a member of that cult, but not a screamer. In the years before the Mets, true cultists would make the long journey to Philadelphia to see Mays play. I stayed home. Say, just, that I am a junior member of the cult. I appreciate Willie Mays very much, and let it go at that.

And now I'll tell you when he gave me my greatest thrill.

It was the 1964 All-Star game, at Shea Stadium in New York. For the first time, I had taken my three sons—ages seven, eight and ten—to see the National and American League All-Stars. For the first time, I had them all together to watch Willie Mays. They all appreciated Mays, though they loved Mickey Mantle and had strong tendencies toward the Yankees. They had heard me rave about Willie Mays enough, and hadn't quite believed me. Now they wanted to be shown.

This is a man who is always at his best in All-Star games, who has a batting average of .390, who has broken up games with his bat and base-running, and rescued games with his glove, and holds various All-Star game records (the most hits, most runs scored, etc.). Well, it wasn't one of Willie's greatest All-Star games. But this one was a little different.

In the sixth inning, the American League had runners on first and second and Brooks Robinson came up and lashed one into the alley between right and center. Mays, running with the wind, dove headlong through the air, and the ball just missed his outstretched glove. It went for a triple, and two runs.

In the seventh, Rocky Colavito rocketed one to the left-center and again Willie Mays flew for it. And again he just missed.

But there were some that should have been hits that Willie caught. "When I see a fly ball coming, I figure I gotta chance to get it." It is a philosophy that has always worked well for Mays. In nine innings he had made seven putouts, and that had tied an All-Star record for center fielders.

But now it was the bottom of the ninth and the American League led 4-3. There was only one more chance left, with Willie Mays leading off against the Monster, Dick Radatz.

At bat in this thirty-fifth All-Star game, Willie had done nothing. In the second inning he had grounded out. In the fourth inning he had fouled out to Elston Howard. In the sixth inning he had been robbed when shortstop Jim Fregosi made a leaping stab of a Mays line drive. He had no chance to bat in the seventh or eighth because Dick Radatz had come in and retired six straight men, four on strikeouts.

Dick Radatz, the Monster, 6 feet 5 inches, 260 pounds—the great, terrifying fastball relief pitcher of the American League.

"He'll strike out Mays," one of my boys said (they are all skeptics). "You wait and see. The American League's gonna win."

Ungrateful wretch, I thought. "Watch, boys, just watch. You'll see what I mean about Willie Mays."

Radatz went into his little motion—the Watusi step with the right leg, the arms drawing slowly down to the belt buckle—and he fired. Before I could breathe, he had two strikes on Mays.

Then the game began.

The third pitch was in tight and Mays danced back and out of the way. (He once said, "They can throw at me, but I ain't gonna be where they're throwin' when the ball comes." He never is.)

Willie fouled off the next pitch, then another. He was just reaching, just hoping for a piece of the ball, trying to protect himself against the strikeout, waiting for the good pitch. And then Radatz threw another one, high and away. And it started again—Willie staying up there fouling off pitches, refusing to back off.

Then Radatz threw his third ball.

Now 50,000 fans could sense something. Now the juices were stirring. Somehow, Willie Mays had been able to work the count to 3 and 2. He hadn't been able to straighten a Radatz fastball, but he had kept himself alive. He was working the pitcher, maybe tiring the pitcher.

In all, Willie fouled off eight pitches and now you knew who was going to win this duel. The air had suddenly grown heavy for the American League.

Dick Radatz finally threw one a fraction inside and the umpire called it that way—ball four—and Willie Mays was springing to first base.

"Now, watch Mays, watch him, boys," I said. "He might steal."

It is unorthodox baseball for a runner to try and

steal with his team a run behind in the ninth inning and nobody out. But Willie has said, "When I see a base out there, I just want to get it."

On Dick Radatz' first pitch, Willie Mays was off. He slid into second base under the tag, which would have been too late, anyway.

I could have said to my kids, those American League diehards—"I told you so! I told you so!"—but I held my breath and just smiled at them, and maybe nudged the closest one in the ribs. I was feeling very superior, and very mean.

Now Orlando Cepeda was the batter and Dick Radatz seemed bothered by Mays, afraid that Willie might try to steal third. Second-baseman Bobby Richardson played close to the bag. It was a mistake. Cepeda blooped a fly into short right field, close to the line. Richardson could not get to it. Willie was into third when first-baseman Joe Pepitone retrieved the ball. Willie was hanging off the base, just looking, just feeling his way. And Pepitone, nervous about the possibility of Willie breaking for home, threw to the plate. He threw badly. Willie was off, flying down the base line, slashing into home plate with the tying run.

We all knew now that the National League must win this game. Four batters later, with two men on base and two out, Johnny Callison came up and hit one out of the park and it was all over.

They named Callison the most valuable player of the All-Star game, and he deserved it. But as we left Shea Stadium that day, there could be only one hero in our family and his name was Willie Mays. My boys had come around a little. They still love Mickey Mantle and the New York Yankees, but Willie Mays—he belongs, too.

He belongs all right.

He is of course the greatest baseball player still active. He will, unquestionably, go down in baseball history as one of the greatest baseball players who ever lived. He will rank, with Ty Cobb and Babe Ruth, as one of the most colorful ballplayers of all time. For sheer excitement combined with pure perfection, has there ever really been anyone like him?

The Los Angeles Dodgers have a point system to judge ballplayers. It is based on these factors: hitting, hitting with power, speed on the bases, strength and accuracy of the arm, and fielding. "Of all the players we ever rated," said Dodger chief scout Al Campanis, "only one was judged to have a perfect score on every count. Willie Mays."

Perfection. But more. "He is," wrote one baseball observer, "the very meaning of baseball, the unbounding joy, the innocent muscled youth that makes the game a constant American theme."

Willie Mays is older now but that description remains true. Even now, in the twilight of his career, he still epitomizes for many the meaning, the essence of baseball.

Before his career is over, he will be the greatest righthanded home run hitter in history, and the greatest home run hitter ever, except for Babe Ruth, whose lifetime mark of 714 seems just out of reach for Willie. But home runs speak only part of the story. At one time or other in his career, Willie has led his league in almost all categories—in batting, in triples, in home runs, in runs scored, in slugging percentage, in total bases, in stolen bases (four years in a row), and in outfield assists. In fielding, in catching a ball and throwing out batters, there simply has been no one like him.

And the man, the personality, rides hand in hand with the athlete. In his youth, Willie used to come home from the ballpark and go out on the streets of Harlem and play stickball with the boys. He was the Say-Hey Kid once. He is no more. Life has bounced him around. He has had financial troubles. He made a marriage that did not work out. He is a Negro, and that is two strikes right there. He has changed some over the years, hardened some. But watching him play ball, even today, you still see the joy in his soul. And listening to him talk, you still hear that joy.

And you think of how it all began.

Willie Howard Mays was born in Westfield, Alabama, on May 6, 1931. Willie's grandfather, Walter Mays, had been a pitcher for a local semi-pro team. Willie's father was an active semi-pro player. His mother, Ann Mays, had been a track star in high school. The heritage was there. When he was fourteen months old, Willie's dad was rolling a ball to Willie across the floor of their home and Willie would roll it back. And when the father got tired and quit, his son would cry and cry.

But there was precious little time for this kind of activity in the Mays home. Times were hard and Willie Howard Mays, Sr. worked long hours in a steel mill in Birmingham, Alabama, and if he earned $2,000 a year it was a good year.

At the age of three, Willie's father and mother parted and he went to live with his Aunt Sarah in

Fairfield, Alabama. Aunt Sarah raised the boy and became an important influence in his life, but his father managed to see him once in a while and play ball with his son. When Willie was three, they used to have catches. They would play pepper, too, with Willie's father hitting groundballs at the boy from about fifteen feet, and Willie beginning to learn the scooping-up technique which is one of his trademarks today.

Willie's mother married again and she had ten children by her second husband, and she died in 1953 giving birth to her tenth child. Willie today is close to his half brothers and sisters, and he has never forgotten his mother.

But sport was the dominating influence in his life as a youngster. He was a natural, Willie was. He could do everything, but even when he was starring in baseball, basketball and football in high school, he knew that being a natural wasn't enough. "You got to practice," he said. "First you got to love the game so you'll want to practice, but you got to go out and try to do different things and you got to practice doing them."

Willie did. When he was only six years old he would go out with a fungo bat and hit himself fly balls and then chase them down. At Fairfield Industrial High he led all Jefferson County in scoring in basketball, averaging between twenty and twenty-five points a game. He loved football, too. He was a quarterback and his coach, Jim McWilliams, called him "the greatest forward passer I ever saw."

But baseball was his game and he immediately saw baseball as a way out from the poverty of his home life. In 1948 when he was seventeen he signed to play baseball professionally with the Birmingham Black Barons in the Negro National League. Though he had done some pitching in the sandlots and high school, he was an outfielder from the beginning with Birmingham. He was an excellent fielder, but he had not yet developed as a hitter. His manager, Piper Davis, kept telling him, "Willie, you stand too close to the plate. You hide behind your left shoulder like you're peeking at the pitcher."

"What should I do?" young Willie asked.

"Aim on that pitcher," said Davis. "Don't peek at him."

Willie moved back a bit and opened up his stance and in 1949 he hit .316 for the Barons.

And the way he played the game! Baseball had now become a passion with him. One afternoon he was playing pool in a local parlor and the Barons' bus left for the next town without him. Miles later, the bus driver saw a taxi pull alongside. Willie Mays was half out of the window, screaming at the top of his lungs at Piper Davis. "What you gonna do? You gonna leave me? I'm a pro ballplayer, you hear! You can't leave me!"

He was a pro ballplayer all right, a fine one. Birmingham fans appreciated him so much that they presented him with a new Mercury automobile. It was his first car and he drove right down to a gas station and asked for $25 worth of gas.

Now the major-league scouts began to come around. The Yankees scouted him, and rejected him. The Dodgers scouted him, and rejected him. The Braves scouted him, and wanted him, but they attached provisions to the contract they offered. Then two New York Giant scouts, Ed Montagne and Billy Harris, visited the Barons. They had been tipped about the Barons' first baseman, but as soon as they saw Willie perform in center field they forgot all about the other fellow. They recommended the Giants pay Willie a bonus of $6,000 to sign a contract with Trenton, New Jersey, in the Class Interstate League.

Willie reported to Trenton and his first twenty-two times up, he couldn't get a hit. He was disgusted. He said to the manager, "How'm I gonna hit this pitching?"

"Don't worry about it," said the manager, Bill Mc-Kechnie, Jr. "You don't strike me as the worrying kind."

"I'm not."

"Well, don't start in now. Just go up there and take your swings."

Willie did, batted .353 in eighty games and earned a promotion to Minneapolis, the Giants' top farm. Class AAA.

He had played in only thirty-five games with Minneapolis when scout Hank DeBerry sent this report back to New York:

"Sensational. Is probably the outstanding player in all the minor leagues now . . . Hits all pitches and hits to all fields. Hits the ball where it's pitched as good as any player seen in many days. Everything he does is sensational. He has made the most spectacular catches, runs and throws with the best of them. Naturally, has some faults, some of which are: charges low-hit balls too much, runs a bit with his head down. There have been a few times when his manager needed a rope. When he starts somewhere, he means to get there, hell bent for election. Slides hard, plays hard. He is sensational and just about as popular with local fans as he can be—a real knockout. . . This player is the best prospect in America. It was a banner day for the Giants when this boy was signed!"

The word on Willie Mays, just turned twenty years old.

He was sitting one afternoon in a Minneapolis movie theatre when he was paged and told to go back to his hotel and look up his manager, Tommy Heath. Willie rushed back to his hotel and Heath told him the good news—"You're going up to the big leagues."

Willie's reaction was a little odd. "They don't want me," he said. "I can't play that kind of ball."

"Of course you can," said Heath.

"No, I can't," said Mays.

Later that night Mays got a call from the manager of the New York Giants, Leo Durocher. Durocher came right to the point.

"Willie, pick up your tickets, hop a plane and I'll see you here tomorrow."

"You're makin' a mistake," Willie said. "I'm not good enough."

"What you hitting?" Leo asked.

There was a slight pause. "Four seventy seven."

Durocher chuckled. "Do you think you could hit half that for me?"

Willie was on his way. He played his first major-league game for the Giants in Philadelphia on the night of May 25, 1951. He was nineteen days past his twentieth birthday. He stood 5 feet 11 inches and weighed 180 pounds. He had a young, happy, smiling face. He batted against a righthander named Bubba Church and he went hitless in five trips.

It was all right, though. He had a sympathetic room-mate in outfielder Monte Irvin. Durocher had told Irvin, "Take good care of him. He's my boy."

Monte did. When Willie failed to get a hit in his first twelve times up, Monte was there to console him, to keep up his spirits. "It's only a slump," Willie said, as though to reassure himself. "I been taking a lot of pitches because I want to see what they throw up there. Now I've found out. They're throwing the same stuff I was belting in Minneapolis. Not many curves, either. They're giving me the stuff I want."

On May 28, Willie finally got his first hit—a home run over the left field roof at the Polo Grounds off Warren Spahn. Then he went thirteen times more without a hit and his average plummeted to .039. It has never been lower. He began to find his eye, he began to hit, and by June 15 he was batting .315. He was on his way.

So were the Giants. When Willie reported to New York, the Giants were in fifth place. By August 11 they were up to second, but still a distant thirteen games behind the Brooklyn Dodgers.

On August 15, the Giants met the Dodgers at the Polo Grounds and that was the day Willie Mays made the first of his miracle plays.

It happened in the eighth inning, the score tied 1-1, the Dodgers' Carl Furillo at bat with runners on first and third and one out.

Furillo hit a long drive into right center. Willie broke at the crack of the bat and, running at full speed, speared the ball. Billy Cox, holding on third, sprinted for home. Willie made the catch facing the right-field line, an almost impossible position from which to throw for a righthander. Willie caught the ball, planted his left foot, pivoted *away* from the play, his back to the plate, then came full around, violently, and let the ball fly. The ball cut through the cutoff man, cut through on a line to catcher Wes Westrum who put the tag on the amazed Billy Cox as Cox slid into the plate. Carl Furillo, who had hit the ball, said afterward in wonder, "It was an impossible play."

But Willie had made the impossible, as he was to do time after time, and the Giants were on their way. They made their historic stretch run, including a sixteen-game winning streak, and when the regular season was over, the Giants had tied the Dodgers for first place.

That Dodger-Giant playoff will always be remembered for what Bobby Thomson did in the third and deciding game, the last-second Horatio Alger home run that won the pennant for the Giants. And the World Series had to be antic-climactic. The Yankees beat the Giants in six games and Willie batted only .182, but it had been some season for the rookie.

It had been a delightful season all around. He had hit .274, with twenty home runs, sixty-eight runs batted in and twelve important assists from the outfield. But it had been more than that. Willie had set a new style for baseball. On the field he set off sparks lashing at pitches, diving headlong into bases, running out of his cap on the field, making his patented basket catches, throwing like Wonder Boy. Off the field he was the same.

His personality, his enthusiasm, his youth, his good cheer—all of this had relaxed the team. He called Monty Irvin "Roomie," and Irvin called Willie,

"Buck." Willie couldn't remember names (just like Babe Ruth) and everyone was "Say-Hey!" to Willie. He would go out on the road and down heaping quantities of ice cream, pie à la mode, soda pop, and iced tea. He would kid his teammates. He'd stick his finger in their ears so that when they saw him coming they would instantly cover their ears with their hands. Sometimes, in the morning when Monte Irvin was trying to sleep late after a night game, Willie would throw cold water in his face to wake him. And when Willie read the papers about himself, read where a writer had compared him to Tris Speaker or Babe Ruth, he'd poke Irvin and say, "See this, Roomie. That's funny stuff. Real funny stuff."

He and Monte Irvin were very close and in the spring of 1952, Willie cried for Irvin. It happened in an April exhibition game. Irvin had walked and Willie singled and Monte raced into third base and slid in and tore up his right ankle so badly he couldn't look at it. Willie ran over and tears poured down his cheeks and he began beating his fists against the ground as he cried out, "I hadda go get that hit. I wish I hadn't gotten it. What did I have to get that hit for?"

That was Willie Mays in 1952, a boy still young in heart, with simple emotions. Two years in the Army did nothing to change him, but he was able to play baseball in the Army for the Fort Eustis, Virginia team and he hit .420 in 1952 and .389 in 1953. In 1954 he was back in training camp and he had to prove himself all over again.

That spring Cleveland manager Al Lopez watched Willie in batting practice. Lopez, one of the game's most respected men, said, "Mays is a .270 hitter who might hit .300 if they teach him to bunt down the third-base line."

Did Willie hear Lopez? He must have in view of the way he played that year. On the final day of the season, the National League batting title was a three-way battle between Mays, teammate Don Mueller and the Dodgers' Duke Snider. Willie faced Robin Roberts of the Phillies, then one of baseball's greatest pitchers. In four at-bats, he singled to left, doubled and tripled to right-center. Mueller went two-for-six to finish with a .342 average. Snider went two-for-four and his average was .341. Willie finished at .345 to win the batting title at the age of twenty-three.

It had been a phenomenal year for Willie. He led the league in triples with thirteen, in slugging percentage with .667. He hit forty-one homers, drove in 110 runs, scored 119. And he would be voted the National League's Most Valuable Player.

But first there was the World Series.

The Giants, led by Mays, had won the National League pennant with ninety-seven victories, but their American League opponents, the Cleveland Indians, had won a record-breaking 111 games. The first World Series game was played in the Polo Grounds and Willie set right out to put Cleveland manager Al Lopez' mind at ease.

It was the top of the eighth and the score was tied, 2-2, and the Indians were threatening. Larry Doby was on second base and Al Rosen on first, none out, and Vic Wertz up at bat. Vic had been a one-man offense thus far— a triple, a double and two singles. He remained hot when he lashed into a Don Liddle pitch and sent it screaming on a line out toward the deepest part of center field, where the 460-foot sign beckoned.

At the crack of the bat, Willie Mays turned around and started racing the ball. With his back to the plate, running like a scared jackrabbit, Mays ran on and on until his feet touched the cinder warning track, ran on close to the fence. Then, at the last desperate moment, he raised his glove over his left shoulder and the ball nestled there, safe and unharmed.

Mays spun around, his cap falling off, his right hand yanking the ball from the glove, and threw it 350 feet to Davey Williams at second.

As Willie trotted back to the Giant dugout, teammate Monte Irvin patted him on the rear end and said, "Nice catch, Buck. I didn't think you were gonna get it."

Willie grinned. "I had it all the way, Roomie. I had it all the way."

That catch—quite possibly the most famous in World Series history—had to demoralize the Indians. The Giants went on to win the game and sweep the Indians in four games.

And so the Willie Mays parade had begun, the procession that will surely lead him some day to Cooperstown, New York and the Hall of Fame. In 1955 Willie batted .319, led the league in homers with fifty-one, and in assists with twenty-three, and tied in triples with thirteen. In 1956 he dropped a bit to .296 but began his reign as base-stealing leader in the National League, a reign that was to last four straight years.

In 1957, his last year in New York, Willie batted .333 and led the league in triples with twenty. Then it was San Francisco and it took awhile for the San Francisco fans to appreciate his talents. In those early years with the Giants he did a little bit of everything. In 1958 he batted .347 and led the league in runs scored with 121. In '59 he hit .313. In '60 he hit .319 and led the league in hits with 190. In 1961 it was .308, forty home runs and a league-leading 129 runs scored. Every year he led the league in something.

But it was more than that. It was the way he did things. Maybe it was a clutch home run, or driving the pitcher crazy on the bases, or one of those impossible fielding plays.

There was one on Roberto Clemente at Forbes Field in Pittsburgh, the ball heading for the light tower and Mays leaping at the last second for the catch. There was the sinking line drive hit by Ed Bouchee, Willie burrowing on his belly to make the shoestring catch. There was the one against Bobby Morgan of the Dodgers, a Mays favorite. Morgan hit a line drive into left-center. Willie, running far to his right, leaped through the air so that his body was stretched full out and parallel to the ground, catching the ball with the tip of his glove and then falling so heavily that his right elbow caved into his solar plexus, knocking him unconscious. But when they ran out to him he had the ball tucked under his body, tucked against his chest, proof that it had never touched the ground.

In 1964 he made another impossible catch. This one was in Philadelphia and it was a close game with the Giants leading 1-0 when Ruben Amaro smashed one deep to right-center. Listen to this description by a Mays specialist, Arnold Hano:

"Mays whirled and ran. He must have run close to a

hundred feet. He ran as far as he could and then he leaped, left hand extended, his face two feet from the boards. He clutched the ball with that extended gloved hand, and then he threw his legs straight out so that he wouldn't hit the fence with his face. He hit it with his stiffened legs, as the rest of him smashed the fence, and he landed on his back."

For a moment he lay stunned. Then he rose and flipped the ball to outfielder Jim Hart and the Philadelphia fans stood up and cheered; cheered him for five minutes.

The cheering has never stopped. You could go on and on. On April 30, 1961, at Milwaukee, he hit four home runs off three Braves' pitchers. He called that one his greatest day.

The Giants won another pennant in 1962 and Willie helped them with his .304 average, his league-leading forty-nine home runs, his 141 runs batted in.

And, though age was stealing up on him, he was not slowing down, although since 1962 he has had a series of inexplicable collapses and brief fainting spells. But they have not stopped him. His managers began resting him here and there and that was all, and that was all he asked.

In 1963 he hit .314 with thirty-eight home runs and 103 runs batted in. In 1964 he was even better. His average slipped to .296 but he led the league with forty-seven home runs, and he scored 121 runs and drove in 111.

He was no longer the Say-Hey Kid. He was older, more set in his ways. He was a man now, a man everyone looked up to. In 1965 when Juan Marichal had that ugly fight with Dodger catcher John Roseboro and struck Roseboro over the head with a bat, it was Willie who was the chief peacemaker. It was Willie, too, who had tears in his eyes and who came over to Roseboro, the enemy, and said, "Johnny, Johnny. I'm so sorry."

The year 1965 was probably the most remarkable of his life. He did not have complete fulfillment because his Giants just failed to catch the Dodgers. But it had not been Willie's fault.

Here is what he did.

In the month of August alone, he hit seventeen home runs, making a new National League record. When the Giants were streaking to fourteen straight wins, Willie was the driving force, batting .315 in that period, with seventeen homers and sixteen runs batted in.

He hit his 500th home run in 1965. And on September 28 he played his 2000th big-league game and hit his fifty-first home run, tying his season's high. He hit fifty-two home runs all told, batted .317, drove in 117 runs, and won his second Most Valuable Player award. He was thirty-four years old and never better.

And now in the twilight of his career, earning the greatest salary any ballplayer had ever received (an estimated $135,000), the only question was how long could he go on, and then what? "I think if I'm lucky and take care of myself," he said at the end of the 1965 season, "I can play another four or five years. And when I can't play, I want to be in baseball in some way, maybe like Stan Musial is."

Willie knows he can make contributions after his career is over. "Let me tell you something," he said to sportswriter Milton Gross. "I don't care what other people think or say, but there ain't no job I can't do in baseball."

Look back over the fifteen years. Look back at what he has done in baseball. How can you doubt Willie Mays?

Red Grange

> A streak of fire, a breath of flame,
> Eluding all who reach and clutch;
> A gray ghost thrown into the game
> That rival hands may never touch;
> A rubber bounding, blasting soul
> Whose destination is the goal—
> Red Grange of Illinois!

A STREAK of fire. A gray ghost. A galloping ghost. That was it—the Galloping Ghost. Leave it to Grantland Rice, the resident sporting poet of the 1920's and 1930's to find the right imagery for the right athlete. Grantland Rice was the premier sportswriter of those years but chances are he will be most remembered for the nicknames he pinned on great athletes.

It was the era for nicknames. If you notice, now, in our generation, none of our superstars really have extravagant, colorful, flashing nicknames. Sandy Koufax is Sandy Koufax. Mickey Mantle is Mickey Mantle.

Jimmy Brown is Jimmy Brown. Willie Mays is Willie Mays. The last real nickname given to a superstar was for Ted Williams—the Splendid Splinter. But that one never really caught on, and it certainly didn't compare to the Galloping Ghost.

The Galloping Ghost was a name suited to the times —the midpoint of the Roaring Twenties, the first Golden Age of sports, when it was Babe Ruth in baseball, Jack Dempsey in boxing, Bill Tilden in tennis, Earl Sande in horseracing, Bobby Jones in golf and Red Grange, the super football hero. The Galloping Ghost suited both the era and the man who wore the name.

Harold "Red" Grange was the Galloping Ghost in every conceivable way. The only football player before his time who could match Grange was Jim Thorpe, and Thorpe's style was different. Jim Thorpe was a powerhouse. He was made of steel. He excelled out of sheer, brute, instinctive power. Red Grange was a man of finesse, a stylist. He was a runner, possibly the most sensational broken-field runner of all times. Listen to what Bob Zuppke, Grange's coach at Illinois, said of his prize student:

"When he got that football under his arm, he was something out of this world. He was the shiftiest runner I've ever seen. He had a hip action, a way of faking you out of position that you wouldn't believe. He was the most relaxed player I ever saw. He reminded me of a leopard that could lay on a limb all day until his prey came along. He knew how to save himself for action that meant something."

Red Grange was unique in his day. Since his day we have had players like Tom Harmon, Whizzer White,

Steve Van Buren, Glenn Davis and Jimmy Brown. But if Grange was not the best of the lot, he certainly was the first, and that was why he became celebrated as the Galloping Ghost.

Go through all of Red Grange's college games, try to pick the one that gets to the essence of Red Grange. It is difficult because there were so many patented Red

Grange performances. Certainly, he put on his greatest one-man show as a junior against Michigan when he ran for five incredible touchdowns. He himself remembers the Chicago game that same year as his greatest. But in almost every game, Grange did something to strike a superlative response from sportswriters who were watching, and from the fans in the stands.

But one game does stand out. One game, we think, sums it all up about the Galloping Ghost.

It was the fourth game of Red Grange's senior year, against the University of Pennsylvania—Red Grange's first invasion of the East.

Remember, in those days, eastern football was supreme. Eastern sportswriters like George Trevor and Damon Runyan had an inclination to look down their noses at the western brand of football. In 1925 they were especially skeptical of Red Grange. Sure, he had been named first-string on Walter Camp's All-American team two years in a row. But this was a new season. Illinois had already been beaten by Nebraska, Iowa and Michigan, and Grange had scored only one touchdown in those three games. Could it be that he had reached his height as a twenty-one-year-old junior and that was the reason he was now on the downgrade?

Pennsylvania, too, was a powerhouse in the East. In 1924 Penn had lost only one game while scoring 203 points to 30 for the opposition. And they had one more thing in their favor. The day before the Illinois game it rained in Philadelphia. It rained, and rained, and rained. If Penn's awesome line couldn't stop Grange, then surely a muddy field would.

The rain continued the day of the game, and

through the game itself. Red Grange remembers, "My old-style pants and jersey absorbed about ten pounds of water and mud. Obviously, carrying that extra poundage was a heavy handicap."

Some handicap.

The game was five minutes old and Illinois had the ball on its own 45. Red Grange, at halfback, took the direct snap from center and with that super-fast start of his, flashed into the right side of the big Penn line. A Penn tackle jarred him in the legs. Red shuddered, stopped for a split second, then picked up again. He broke through the line, cut right towards the sidelines, then, as a defensive back tried to hem him in, knifed back towards the middle of the field. And then he was alone, running at a gallop in the style about which Grantland Rice wrote, "as Nurmi runs, as Dempsey moves, with almost no effort, as a shadow flits and drifts and darts."

It was a 55-yard touchdown run and the great crowd of 55,000 at Franklin Field in Pennsylvania, that great crowd that had come to be shown, stood up as one and cheered.

But Red wasn't finished.

Minutes after the touchdown, he caught a Penn kick deep in his own territory and bolted downfield. It was another virtuoso performance of dodging, whirling and shedding tacklers. He went fifty-five yards before he was hit. Three plays later he took the ball in for the score.

From then on, the skeptical, sophisticated crowd was all for the Redhead from Illinois. The Reverend Billy Graham couldn't have converted them the way Red did. Every time No. 77 carried the ball the cry went up, "There goes the Redhead!"

The Redhead went all afternoon. He scored three touchdowns and was largely responsible for the fourth. Twice he roared to sixty-yard runs. In thirty-six tries he made 363 yards. Illinois beat Penn 24-2 and Red Grange, with ten pounds of mud, and a burdensome reputation, on his back, was all he was supposed to be. The crowd went out muttering to themselves, "If he's this good on a muddy field, what's he like on a dry one?"

And up in the pressbox one of those cynical eastern writers, George Trevor, sat stunned, unable to type out his story. Finally, twenty minutes later, he collected his thoughts and he wrote of Red Grange:

"He has the knack of shortening or lengthening his stride instantaneously; he has the speed to outsprint the fastest defensive back, the guile to sidestep the adroitest tackler, the strength to straightarm the most powerful adversary."

Red Grange. The Galloping Ghost. In three years for Illinois, he ran for 3,637 yards, a school record that held until 1965, broken finally by fullback Jim Grabowski. In three years he scored thirty-one touchdowns.

He was, as a collegian, the most talked-about, written-about and photographed player of his time. And then he went into professional football, and if one man deserves credit for making pro football the game it is today, that man is Harold Edward "Red" Grange.

But that is getting far ahead of our story. The story properly begins in the little rustic town of Forksville, Pennsylvania. Harold Edward Grange was born in

Forksville on June 13, 1903. His father was a foreman for the Pennsylvania Lumber Company. His mother died when he was five years old and it was then that his father Lyle Grange decided to go west and settle in Wheaton, Illinois, where four of his brothers were already living.

Harold Grange was the third in a family of four children. The girls, Norma and Mildred were the oldest. Red's younger brother Garland later played end for Illinois. Red's dad joined the local police force in Wheaton and eventually became Chief. Red went to school where he began to develop his interest in athletics.

He started playing football when he was nine years old. He played at first against the advice of the family doctor who thought that Red had a weak heart. The doctor was mistaken because Red kept on playing football, baseball and basketball, and participating in all the track and field events he could. And the more he played, the better he became.

Red Grange was a natural, but he had to work at it, too. And Red Grange was a hard worker. When he was fourteen he worked on an uncle's farm from dawn to dusk. It was hard, backbreaking labor. As a fifteen year old, weighing less than 140 pounds, he was so strong that he won a dollar from a local iceman for lifting a seventy-five pound cake of ice on his shoulder. The iceman, Luke Thompson, promptly gave Red a job. From then on, every summer while he was in high school and college, Red worked on Luke Thompson's ice wagon.

By the time he was ready for college he was strong and fit—5 feet 10 inches, 170 pounds, with rippling,

muscular shoulders, legs like corded wood and a sup-
ple disposition. His freckled face was sunny, his hair
was really more of a burnt blond than red, but it had a
red glint when the sun shone on it.

And by the time he was ready for college, he had a
reputation.

He earned it spectacularly at Wheaton High with
his performance in four sports. He was a *sixteen-*
letterman at Wheaton. As a freshman he was already a
basketball all-star. In baseball he did so well he received an offer from the old Boston Braves. In track he
ran the 100-yard dash, the 220, the low hurdles, the
high jump and running broad jump. He was a state
champion in three different events.

And in football, nobody had ever seen anything like
Red Grange. In his three years he scored 532 points—
on seventy-five touchdowns and eighty-two conversions.

But he never received a scholarship offer. This was
1922 and the athletic scholarship hadn't been invented. But Wheaton was only twenty-five miles from
Chicago, and Illinois was situated just outside Chicago, and the boy next door, George Dawson, was at
Illinois. So Red Grange decided that Illinois was for
him.

Bob Zuppke, the head coach of the Illini, couldn't
have been happier. But he knew that Red wasn't yet a
finished player. "As a freshman," Zuppke said, "Red
was a sidelines runner. He was always stepping out of
bounds."

Zuppke finally lost patience with Grange and he
told the freshman coach, Burt Ingwersen, "Bench that

fellow and put in a man who can give the varsity some practice."

It was then that Zuppke figured how to straighten Red out. He devised a gigantic S, which he drew on the blackboard before every game to remind Red of how he was expected to run. In practice Red would have to run through the S time and time again. He would swing wide around his own right end, cut back to his left, and then near the end of the run, veer to the right again.

This wasn't Red's natural style but he worked hard at it and by the time he was a sophomore he could run through the S blindfolded.

In his first varsity game, against Nebraska Red exploded onto the nation's consciousness. He broke loose for touchdown runs of thirty-five, sixty and twelve yards. The headline in the Chicago *Tribune* the next day read: "GRANGE SPRINTS TO FAME." It was true.

Later that season against Northwestern he showed his verve on defense. In the second quarter, Red intercepted a pass on his own ten and roared ninety yards for the touchdown. He scored three that day in Illinois' 29-0 rout of Northwestern.

His most satisfying sophomore performance came on a most fitting day. On November 3, 1933, Illinois opened its new $2,000,000 stadium against the University of Chicago. Red Grange was in a festive mood.

The Illini won a hard-fought game, 7-0. Without Red Grange they wouldn't have won at all. Time after time Red kept Chicago off-balance with his blinding runs. In the first quarter he tore off a forty-two-yard gallop. In the third quarter he ran sixty yards. But still no score. Finally, Illinois began to move from its own thirty-seven.

Red Grange and teammate Wally McIlwain took turns hitting the line. Red for five, then a twenty-three yard burst, then a fifteen-yard end run. And now the ball was on the Illinois seven.

McIlwain hit the center of the line for two yards, and now it was Red's turn. No S run here. He went right through center. Chicago linemen touched him but couldn't stop him until he was in the end zone for the only touchdown of the game.

At the end of that sophomore year, Red had scored twelve touchdowns and gained 1,260 yards. And Walter Camp put him on his first All-America team.

Bob Zuppke was of course overjoyed about Grange, and about the prospect of having him for two more years. "I once made a trip to the Kaibab Forest on the edge of the north rim of the Grand Canyon," Zup said once, "and as a deer ran out onto the grass plains, I said, 'There goes Red Grange.'

"The freedom of movement was so similar to Red's. Red had that indefinable something that the hunted wild animal has—uncanny timing and the big brown eyes of a royal buck. I sketched a team around him like the complementary background of a painting. Those were not great teams that Grange played for. But they fitted around him, helped to set him off."

In 1924, Red's junior year, the team set him off perfectly.

Everyone knew that only one game counted on that schedule—the Michigan game. In 1923 the two teams had not met. Each had gone undefeated, each had won five games against no defeats in Big Ten competition, which meant sharing the Conference crown. The supreme moment of truth for Michigan, for Illinois, for Red Grange, would come on October 18, 1924, at Champaign-Urbana, Illinois.

Both teams played their first two games without mishap. Michigan beat Miami of Ohio and Michigan State. In its opener against Nebraska, Illinois won but Red Grange did not score. Against Butler, Illinois won again, 40-10, and Red scored twice—on a fifteen and forty-eight yard runs.

Illinois had looked impressive all right, but Michigan—why Michigan under Fielding Yost hadn't been beaten since 1921. And Michigan wasn't one bit afraid of Red Grange. Fielding Yost told the press, "Mister Grange will be a carefully watched young man anytime he takes the ball. There will be just about eleven clean, hard tacklers headed for him at the same time. I know he's a great runner, but great runners usually have the hardest time gaining ground when they are met by special preparation."

What was the special preparation Yost was devising for Grange? It was startling in its simplicity. Yost knew about Zuppke's S design. The answer to it was to hem Red in before he could make his diagonal cut to the sidelines. Let him run to the sidelines and then pinch in on him, trap him, smash him there, toss him out of bounds, make it impossible for him to cut back inside.

There were 67,000 people in Illinois' stadium, the largest crowd ever to watch a game in the Midwest up to that time. They were poised on the edge of their seats, at the point of hysteria, their eyes on one person only—the man wearing No. 77.

Bob Zuppke had put in one innovation for the

game. He sent his team on the field without long stock-ings. It was the first time this had ever been done. Yost was enraged. He called it "another one of Zuppke's damned tricks." He had an official check to make sure that the players' legs were not greased. They were not, but the psychological damage had been done. A Mich-igan player said afterwards, "As soon as we saw the Illinois players bare-legged we became conscious of the heat, and our own legs became heavy as lead."

Michigan lined up to kick off to Illinois. Red stood back there with Wally McIlwain. The kicker, Herb Steger, was told to kick away from Grange.

But a strong wind was blowing that day and the kick misfired and Red took the low line drive on his five-yard line.

He waited for his blockers to form in front of him and then headed for the right sidelines. A clutch of Michigan tacklers descended on him, ready to execute their coach's strategy. But when Red tightroped along the right boundary line, he immediately cut sharply to his left, making the cut before a Michigan tackler could touch him.

He crossed the whole field, to the left sideline, then ran a straight course for about twenty yards, then cut back sharply again, heading for the right corner of the goal line. The Michigan safety-man made a desperate dive but it was too late. The Redhead had scored on a ninety-five-yard run.

Immediately, Michigan decided to kick off again. Red took it, but was dropped on the twenty.

After an exchange of punts, Illinois had the ball on its own thirty-three. From a deep box formation, the pass from center went back to Grange. He veered towards the Michigan left end. Suddenly, he cut back over that position and headed for the far sidelines. The entire wave of Michigan tacklers had moved toward the left with him and now Red was alone, with a wall of Illinois blockers between him and Michigan. He accelerated and steamed sixty-seven yards for the touchdown.

Michigan still remained unconvinced and elected to kick off once more. Red took the ball on his own forty-four, followed his usual S to the right, let the Michigan tacklers close in on him against the sidelines, then once again cut sharply away. He straightened out at mid-field and went into fourth gear and left everyone behind him. It was another masterpiece of skill and timing. How did he do it? His coach once tried to explain. Said Zuppke:

"When Red Grange ran a play, his imagination pictured the part and duties of every one of his teammates. Due to his panoramic view and quick thinking, he had the ability to spot instantly where the most effective blocking would carry him."

That glorious afternoon under a blue-gray Illini sky, with the crowd in the stands chanting the Illinois fight song, "We're Loyal To You Illinois," the Red-head was immortal.

Still in the first period, he ran his patented play from the Michigan forty-four. He swept end, made his cut, drew clear and flashed over the goal line without a human laying a finger on him.

In twelve minutes he had scored four touchdowns.

In twelve minutes he had run 262 yards.

And it was then his coach took him out. "Why?" he asked Bob Zuppke.

"Because," Zuppke answered, "no Michigan man has laid a hand on you yet. I want you to come out unsoiled."

Actually, Zuppke said later, "I didn't want him to get hurt. And I didn't want to leave the impression that Michigan was a weak team. I wanted Grange's feat to mean something."

But Grange got back in the game later, and scored his fifth touchdown on a twelve-yard run. So Illinois won 39-14 and Grange had accounted for all six touchdowns. He had gained 402 yards in twenty-one carries, and completed six passes for seventy-eight more yards.

Everybody remembers Red Grange for that game; that one was probably the crowning achievement of his life. But there were others. There was one three weeks later.

To this day Red Grange is proudest of the game he played against the University of Chicago as a junior. "It was the most rugged game I ever played in college," Red said. "They really had a good club, and they were out to get us. They had us down, too—but we got back up."

Indeed they did. It was 14-0, Chicago, before Red Grange was even to get his hands on the ball. Amos Alonzo Stagg, the Chicago coach, had a strategy that was artistic in its simplicity. Chicago would practice ball control, would not permit Illinois to get the ball, and that meant not letting Grange get the ball.

Finally, though, Illinois did get the ball and started to move. The Chicago line, mindful of what had happened to Michigan, sealed off the ends, so Red had to make his way through the middle. In one sustained drive with Red carrying the ball on trap attacks through the widely spaced line and throwing an occasional pass (and catching another), Illinois finally scored.

But Chicago came right back and took a 21-7 lead. Then, with two minutes left in the half, Grange led the way again. He carried the ball nine times and caught two passes. Illinois scored to make it 21-14.

In the third period the Galloping Ghost struck with all his fury.

He took the ball on the Illinois twenty, on the direct snap from center in Bob Zuppke's single-wing formation. He hit off tackle, his legs churning through a mass of tough Chicago defenders. Somehow, he broke clear. Now he was all alone, racing by himself toward the Chicago goal line, with only the whistle of the wind screeching in his ears. He raced on alone, exultant, crossing the goal line free and clear and fulfilled.

The game ended that way, 21-21, but Red Grange had nothing to be ashamed of.

He had nothing to be ashamed of that entire year. When it was over he had scored thirteen touchdowns and gained 1,164 yards, and of course he was All-American again. He was more. He was now a national hero.

His senior year was something of a disappointment and one reason was that his fame had simply grown out of all proportions. Men fought to talk to him. Girls fought to touch him. The chairman of the board of U.S. Steel invited him to dinner. There was a proposal to nominate him for Congress, and another to name a town after him. "My last year at Illinois," Grange told writer W. C. Heinz, "was all confusion. I had no privacy . . . I wasn't able to study or anything."

Red also had the misfortune during his senior year to play with a green, sophomore-dominant team. He scored only six touchdowns in 1925, the last one in his last great game, against Pennsylvania. But his reputation shone brighter than ever. In his last college game against Ohio State, a crowd of 85,000 spectators turned out at Columbus, Ohio. Illinois won the game 14-9 and Red threw a touchdown pass and gained 153 yards on the ground. Every time No. 77 carried the ball he was cheered.

The next day he signed a contract to play professional football.

It came about this way. Red had become friendly with an Illinois promoter, C. C. Pyle, who owned a chain of movie houses. Pyle, whose nickname, for good and sufficient reason, was "Cash 'n Carry," urged Red to turn pro immediately on playing his last game and grab the opportunity while his name still meant so much to so many people.

Professional football was not only ready for Red Grange; it badly needed him. In 1925, the National Football League was in its fifth year with twenty unwieldy teams. All of them were losing money. There simply was no prestige, no glory, no respectability—and thus no customers—attached to professional football. What the game needed was a name and someone to give pro football respectability. And Red Grange was cut out for the job.

So Grange signed with the Chicago Bears and it was a turning point in the fortunes of pro football. Many experts feel that the game would not be what it is today if it hadn't been for Red Grange.

Immediately, he brought screaming, enthusiastic

crowds to the game. In ten days he played five games. His first professional football game came against the Chicago Cardinals in Wrigley Field on Thanksgiving Day, 1925. The stadium was filled to capacity with 36,000 screaming Red Grange fans. But Red had little opportunity as the Cardinals constantly kicked away from him and the game ended in a scoreless tie.

Three days later he was back in action against the Columbia (Missouri) Tigers. Twenty-eight thousand came out to Wrigley Field in a blinding snowstorn. On the following Wednesday Red played at St. Louis. That Saturday he played before 40,000 rain-drenched fans in Philadelphia. The next day he played again; this time in the Polo Grounds in New York City.

If it were possible to point to any one game in the history of pro football and say that it was the game that made pro football, it would have to be the Bears-Giants game in New York. It made the New York Giants, for sure. Tim Mara, owner of the Giants, was $45,000 in the red at the start of the game. "Even with Grange in the lineup," Mara said, "I would have been glad to have seen 25,000 in the stands. Instead, the house was swamped. We drew 70,000 and probably could have got another 70,000 if we'd had room."

The Bears won 19-7. Red Grange carried the ball eleven times for forty-five yards. He completed two of three passes. He caught one. He intercepted a pass and ran it back thirty-five yards for a touchdown. Grange had given the crowd its money's worth, and in turn received $30,000 of the record $143,000.

At the end of those ten days, Grange got a check for $50,000. Later the Bears went on a post-season exhibition tour through the South, and Red earned another

$50,000. In his first three years out of school he grossed almost $1,000,000 from football, motion pictures, vaudeville appearances and endorsements.

He played pro football for ten years. He was never the superman as a pro that he was in college. He suffered disabling injuries to his left arm and right knee that prevented him from flashing his complete college form. He sat out all of 1927 with a bad knee and when he came back he was the first to admit that he was now just "an ordinary halfback."

Ordinary? From 1929 on he had to wear a special brace to keep his knee from falling apart. The brace was constructed of elastic and supported by two steel hinges which extended six inches below the knee and six inches above it. But he played on. He was never what he had been at Illinois, but he was good enough. During his pro career he scored 162 touchdowns and kicked eighty-six conversions for a total of 1,082 points. He was good enough.

In 1935, thirty-two years old, Red played his last game. At one point, in that game against the Giants, he broke into the clear. But he was caught from behind by a slow 230-pound tackle. He knew then that he was finished.

After that Red went into the insurance business and did some broadcasting of football games, but he loved the sport too much to ever completely lose touch. Now in the late years of his life, football is still one of his major interests.

And football has not forgotten Red Grange. The late Steve Owen, an all-pro lineman in his own right, once described Red Grange's pro style as running "like two jackrabbits. I never saw anyone's hips twitch so fast to the right, and then to the left. He was like a cat," Steve Owen marveled, shaking his head. "He always landed running."

Let that be Red Grange's epitaph.

The Author

A L S ILVERMAN, editor-in-chief of *Sport* magazine, makes an avocation of his profession by writing numerous books about competitive sports. He is the author of *Mickey Mantle: Mister Yankee* and *Heroes of the World Series,* both published by Putnam.

Index

All-America (football), 206, 212, 217
All-Stars (baseball), 185–88
All-Stars (NBA), 109, 119
Amateur Athletic Union, 25
American League, 35, 89, 96, 102, 186 ff., 198. *See also* specific clubs
Army, 23–24
Auerbach, Arnold (Red), 105–8, 109, 119
Augusta, Ga., 93–94

Baker, Frank "Home Run," 97
Baltimore (International League), 33–34
Baltimore Colts, 86–87
Baseball, 19, 25–26, 29–31, 33–35, 172, 178–79, 184–203, 210. *See also* specific players and clubs
  World Series, 35–48 *passim*, 196, 198–99
Basketball, 106–26, 172, 174–75, 178
Birmingham Black Barons, 191–93
Blake, Toe, 156, 161, 170–71
Boston, Ralph, 125, 127
Boston Braves, 46, 49
Boston Bruins, 157–59, 164, 167, 170
Boston Celtics, 105–10, 116–23
Boston Red Sox, 34–37
Bowling, 172
Brimsek, Frankie, 164
Brooklyn Dodgers, 195–96, 200, 201–2
Brown, James Nathaniel "Jim," 71–88
  records, 74, 76, 82
  Syracuse, 78–80
Brown, Paul, 80, 82–83
Budge, Don, 139, 140, 152

Cadets, 23–24
Callison, Johnny, 188
Campanis, Al, 189
Campbell, Clarence, 167–68
Carlisle Institute, 14–16, 18–20, 22–25

Carpentier, Georges, 62–63
Carrigan, Bill, 34–36
Chase, Hal, 91–92
Chicago, University of, 211–12, 216
Chicago Bears, 218–20
Chicago Black Hawks, 165
Chicago Cubs, 47–48
Chicago Stags, 116
Class Interstate League, 193
Clay, Cassius, 75–76
Cleveland Browns, 72–74, 80–88
Cleveland Indians, 198–99
Cobb, Ty, 89–105
  Augusta, Ga., 93–94
  Cobb Educational Foundation, 104
  Detroit Tigers, 92, 94–103
  Hall of Fame, 103–4
  records, 89, 96, 102, 103
Collier, Blanton, 83, 87
Combs, Earle, 42, 43
Cousy, Bob, 105–23
  All-Stars, 109, 119
  Boston Celtics, 105–10, 116–23
  Chicago Stags, 116
  Most Valuable Player, 109, 119
  records, 109, 110, 118, 120
Cox, Billy, 195–96

Dallas Cowboys, 72, 84
Davis Cup, 139, 141, 145–51 *passim*
Davis, Piper, 192
DeBerry, Hank, 193–94
Decathlon, 21, 80
Dempsey, William Harrison "Jack," 51–70
  Carpentier bout, 62–63
  champion, 61–67
  Firpo bout, 64–67
  Gibbons bout, 63–64
  Tunney bouts, 67, 68–69
  Willard bouts, 59–61
Detroit Red Wings, 155, 157, 162, 165–70
Detroit Tigers, 92, 94–103
Dickinson, 22–23
Didrikson, Babe. *See* Zaharias, Babe Didrikson

222

Dunn, Jack, 33, 34
Durocher, Leo, 194, 195

Ezinicki, Wild Bill, 163

Field. *See* Track and field
Firpo, Luis, 64–67
Football. *See also* specific players
  and teams
  All-American, 20, 25, 79
  college, 14–15, 18–20, 22–25,
    78–80
  pro, 26–27, 72–76, 80–88
Fuchs, Emil, 49
Furillo, Carl, 195–96

Gibbons, Tommy, 63–64
Gilbert, Brother, 32–33
Golf, 172–73, 178–83
Grange, Harold "Red," 203–21
  All-America, 206, 212, 217
  Illinois, University of, 204–8,
    210–18
  records, 208, 210, 215, 220
  pro, 218–20
Green Bay Packers, 88

Hall of Fame, 103–4, 199
Hammill, Red, 165
Harvard, 14–15, 20
Heath, Tommy, 194
Hockey, 154–71
Holy Cross, 113–15
Houghton, Percy, 14–15
Huggins, Miller, 42–43

Illinois, University of, 204–8, 210–218
International League, 33–34
Irvin, Dick, 155–56, 158, 161, 163
Irvin, Monte, 195, 196–97, 199

Jackson, Shoeless Joe, 99
Johnson, Ban, 97, 101
Johnston, William "Little Bill,"
  143, 144, 146–48

Kearns, Jack, 59, 63–64, 66
Koenig, Mark, 47

La Coste, René, 141, 149, 151
Lacrosse, 79–80
Landis, Kennesaw Mountain, 38–
  39, 45
Laycoe, Hal, 167
Lehigh, 23
Lindsay, Ted, 155, 165–66

Long, Luz, 126–27
Lopez, Al, 197–98
Los Angeles Dodgers, 189
Los Angeles Lakers, 122–23
Los Angeles Rams, 81–82
Loyola of Chicago, 114–15

Mack, Connie, 102, 103
Mara, Tim, 219
Massillon Tigers, 26–27
Mays, Willie Howard, 184–203
  All-Stars, 185–88
  Birmingham Black Barons, 191–
    193
  Hall of Fame, 199
  Minneapolis, 193–94
  Most Valuable Player, 198, 202
  New York Giants, 192–202
  records, 189–90, 198–202 *passim*
  Trenton, 193
  World Series, 186, 198–99
McComb, Col. M. J., 175–76, 178
McGraw, John, 25–26
McLean, Hugh, 166
Meusel, Bob, 38–39, 42, 43
Michigan, University of, 212–16
Milwaukee Braves, 201
Minneapolis (Giants' farm team),
  193–94
Minneapolis (NBA), 121
Montreal Canadiens, 155–71
Morgan, Bobby, 200

National Basketball Association
  (NBA), 109, 110, 120, 121.
  See also specific teams
National Football League, 74, 76,
  82, 86, 218. *See also* specific
  clubs
National Hockey League, 155, 163,
  167–88. *See also* specific clubs
National League, 45, 46, 186 ff.,
  198–202. *See also* specific
  clubs
Negro National League, 192
New York Giants (baseball), 25–
  26, 38, 39, 41, 192–202
New York Giants (football), 85–
  86, 219, 220
New York Highlanders, 92, 100
New York Rangers, 156, 164
New York Yankees, 37–49
Northwestern University, 211

Ohio State, 128, 129 ff.
Owen, Steve, 220–21

Owens, Brick, 36
Owens, Jesse, 124–36
  Olympics, 125–127, 132–35
  records, 125, 126, 127–28, 132

Patterson, Gerald, 145, 146
Pennsylvania, University of, 206–8
Pentathlon, 21
Philadelphia Athletics, 97, 101
Philadelphia Phillies, 200–1
Philadelphia Warriors, 108–9, 121
Pippin, Rodger, 34
Pittsburgh, University of, 20, 23
Pittsburgh Pirates, 42, 49
Prizefighting, 51–70
  million-dollar gates, 62, 64, 67
Pyle, C. C., 218

Radatz, Dick, 186–88
Reardon, Kenny, 160–61
Richard, Maurice, 154–71
  Most Valuable player, 163
  records, 155, 157, 162
  Stanley cup, 157–59, 161, 167, 168, 170
Richards, Vinnie, 143, 144
Rickard, Tex, 62, 64–65
Robertson, Oscar "Big O," 121–22
Rockne, Knute, 26–27
Rocky Mount, N.C., 19
Root, Charlie, 48
Roseboro, John, 201–2
Rucker, Nap, 95
Ruppert, Jake, 42, 48–49
Russell, Bill, 110, 119
Ruth, George Herman "Babe," 29–50, 103
  Baltimore, 33–34
  barnstorming, 38–39
  Boston Braves, 46, 49
  Boston Red Sox, 34–37
  New York Yankees, 37–49
  records, 30, 37, 42, 43, 46, 49
  St. Mary's Industrial Home for Boys, 32–33
  World Series, 35–39 *passim*, 41–48 *passim*

Schmidt, Charlie "Dutch," 98
Senesky, George, 108–9
Sherdel, Willie, 45
Shimizu, Zenzo, 145, 148
Siebert, Earl, 162
Snyder, Larry, 128, 130, 133

Stagg, Amos Alonzo, 216
Stanley Cup, 157–59, 161, 167, 168, 170
St. Louis Cardinals, 42, 44–46
St. Louis Hawks, 120–21
St. Mary's Industrial Home for Boys, 32–33
Swimming, 172
Syracuse (NBA), 117–18
Syracuse University, 23, 178–80

Tennis, 136–53, 172
Thorpe, James Francis "Jim," 11–28, 204
  All-America, 20, 25
  baseball, 16, 20, 25–26
  Carlisle Institute, 14–25
  football, 14–15, 18–20, 22–27
  Olympics, 16, 19, 21–22, 25
  pro, 19, 25–27
  Rocky Mount, N.C., 19, 25
  track and field, 14–16, 21–22
Tilden, Herb, 142
Tilden, William Tatum "Bill," 137–153
  championships, 139, 143, 148–51
  Davis Cup, 139, 141, 148–51
  pro, 151–53
  Wimbledon, 139, 144–46
Track and field, 15–16, 77, 79–80, 128, 129, 135, 172, 176, 210
  Olympics, 21–22, 125–27, 132–135, 172, 176–77
Tunney, Gene, 67, 68–69

Walsh, Ed, 77–78
Warner, Pop, 18–19, 24, 28
West Point, 23–24
Willard, Jess, 52, 59–61
Wimbledon, 139, 144–46
World Series. *See* Baseball

Yankee Stadium, 29–30, 40, 50
Yost, Fielding, 213–14

Zaharias, Babe Didrikson, 171–83
  baseball, 172, 178–79
  basketball, 172, 174–75, 178
  golf, 172–73, 178–83
  Olympics, 172, 176–77
  track and field, 172, 176–77
Zaharias, George, 180 ff.
Zuppke, Bob, 204, 210–17